The Complete Marriage

GREEN CARD KIT

A STEP-BY-STEP GUIDE

Expanded & Updated

TEMPLATES AND TOOLS FOR BECOMING A PERMANENT RESIDENT OF THE UNITED STATES

ZEPHYRUS MEDIA

MARCUS CAMPANA

The Complete Marriage Green Card Kit
Copyright © 2011, 2013 by MARCUS J. CAMPANA

Designed in the USA by Zephyrus Media, LLC
Printed in the USA

Important

If your situation is complex, or, you have significant criminal history, are an illegal alien, or a member of a violent organization, for example, it is wise to hire an immigration attorney. An attorney will help you analyze the facts of your case thoroughly, and will explain all of the benefits for which you may or may not be eligible.

Please be aware that you must qualify to apply for a Green Card. If you file when you're not eligible, the government may consider your filing fraudulent, which results in serious penalties. If you enter the U.S. on a tourist visa with the intention of marrying a U.S. citizen or permanent resident, it is considered visa fraud. If you did enter the U.S. on a temporary visa and then unexpectedly fall in love and get married you may face a challenge in proving this to the USCIS. In such cases the foreign spouse should leave the U.S. and file from home. If you were married while on a temporary visa, you should consult a qualified immigration attorney.

Disclaimer

The purpose of The Complete Marriage Green Card Kit is to provide a basic understanding of the rules, laws, processes and regulations concerning United States immigration marriage-based permanent residence procedures. The kit is sold with the understanding that the author and publisher are not offering or proffering legal advice, but only sharing relevant germane information. If professional legal assistance is necessary, the expertise of a qualified immigration attorney should be consulted. This kit contains information on United States Immigration procedures that are only accurate up to the publishing/printing date as the rules and regulations change frequently. The publisher and author shall not be held liable, nor be responsible to any person, business, group, organization or entity with respect to any loss, hardship or damage caused, or alleged to be caused, directly or indirectly by the information contained in this kit. While this book offers complete and accurate information, mistakes in typography and content are possible.

Part One: GUIDEBOOK
Overview

★ Contents

Time Saving Tips, Tricks & Conventions

Step I: Filing Forms

Step II: Sending it Off

Step III: The Interview

Step IV: Removing Conditions

Part Two: CHECKLISTS

Part Three: EXAMPLE ENTRIES

Part Four: TEMPLATES AND PHOTO GUIDES

The Complete Marriage
GREEN CARD KIT
A STEP-BY-STEP GUIDE

Part One: GUIDEBOOK

Welcome, and congratulations on your marriage! Each year, about 500,000 couples apply for marriage-based Green Cards. The great news is that the government imposes no limits on the number of family based Green Card applications and the majority of them are approved.

The purpose of this kit is to escort you through the tangled process of acquiring a Green Card through your marriage to a United States citizen (or Permanent Resident). This kit will allay many of your fears while serving as a helpful companion for both you and your spouse throughout your path to permanent residency.

The order of the guidebook you're reading is chronological. You can read it from cover to cover, consecutively completing the tasks of each chapter. The bulk of this guidebook consists of example entries and explanations for filling out the required USCIS forms. After an overview, all the information presented will be immediately applicable to the current task.

Synonymous Terms

<u>The following terms are synonymous and are used interchangeably throughout the kit:</u>

Green Card (colloquial term) = Permanent Resident Card (official term)
Alien (in this case) = Foreign Spouse = Alien Beneficiary (formally, this was a common official term but it is now rarely used).

Overview of the Process

Before jumping into the details of filing a marriage based Green Card application, it's helpful to have an overview of the entire process.

The path to permanent residency can be divided into two large stages.

Stage I encompasses the application for a <u>two-year *Conditional* Green Card</u>. This card will expire after two years.

Stage II consists of removing the two-year conditions on the Green Card.

If you have been married for less than two years before beginning Stage I, then you must complete both stages as outlined above; this is the most common path. A diagram of the process appears on the following page:

★ **Note:** if you have been married for more than two years before filing your initial application, it is not necessary to remove conditions because your initial filing will grant you a permanent Green Card.

Process Chart

The most common path to Permanent Residency

Stage I: Initial Filing for a 2-Year (Conditional) Green Card

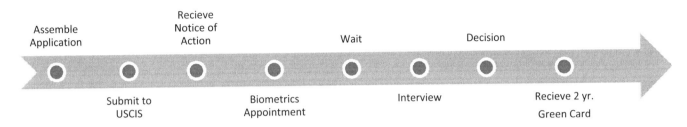

Assemble Application | Recieve Notice of Action | Wait | Decision

Submit to USCIS | Biometrics Appointment | Interview | Recieve 2 yr. Green Card

Stage II: Obtaining a 10-Year Green Card (Removing Conditions)

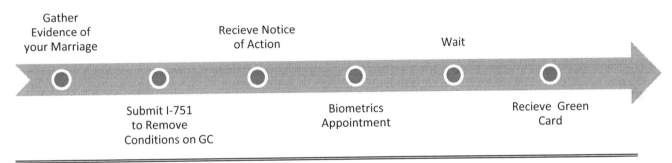

Gather Evidence of your Marriage | Recieve Notice of Action | Wait

Submit I-751 to Remove Conditions on GC | Biometrics Appointment | Recieve Green Card

Time Frame

Steps	Range	Average time	Average Total Time
Complete and Assemble Application	2-15 weeks		5 weeks
Submit Application to USCIS			
Receive Notice of Action (I-797C)	7-28 days	15 days	15 days
Biometrics Appointment Notice	10-50 days	34 days	50 days
Interview Date	3-18 months	5 months	6.5 months
Receive Decision	5-25 days	8 days	6.7 months
Receive 2 yr. Green Card	18-48 days	24 days	7.5 months
Collect Documents for Future Petition		1.5 years	
Submit I-751 (Removal of Conditions)		20 days	
Receive Notice of Action (I-797C)	10-32 days	16 days	
Biometrics Appointment Notice	18-46 days	30 days	1.5 months
Approval Notice (10 Yr. Green Card)	3-9 months	4 months	6 months

The times listed above are approximate and serve only as a rough guide. You may be more fortunate than the average applicant, and complete the process sooner. However, do not be alarmed if the process takes longer than expected. Some cases can take over a year to receive an interview appointment. That being said, if your waiting period exceeds those listed above, you should contact the USCIS to verify that your case is still in good standing.

Contacting USCIS

One effective way to contact USCIS is through INFOPASS, an online USCIS support service.
http://infopass.uscis.gov

You may also call the USCIS directly at 1-800-375-5283.

For more detailed contact info see
http://tinyurl.com/ylmqvlu

Forms to File

The first step, completing and assembling documents, shapes the bulk of this guidebook. The forms that you need are shown below with associated fees:

I-130: Petition for Alien Relative	$420
G-325A: Biographic Information (1 for U.S. Spouse, 2 for Foreign spouse)	No Fee
I-485: Application to Register Permanent Residence or Adjust Status	$1070 Including Biometrics fee
I-864: Affidavit of Support	Included in price of I-485
I-693: Report of Medical Examination and Vaccination Record	Included in price of I-485

Common But Optional Forms

I-765: Application for Employment Authorization	Included in price of I-485
I-131: Application for Travel Document	Included in price of I-485
G-1145: E-Notification of Application/Petition Acceptance	No Fee

Fees are accurate as of 02/2013. Always verify all fees before filing.

The Purpose of Each Form

In the midst of completing each question on each form and attaching dozens of items of evidence, it's easy to get lost in the details.

Below you will find a short summery of the purpose of each form in plain English. This is what each form means to the USCIS:

REQUIRED FORMS

I-130: I am U.S. citizen and I want my foreign-born spouse to live with me in America. Here is proof of our marriage.

G-325A: Here is all my basic biographic data.

I-485: I am a foreign-born spouse of an American citizen and I want to live in America with him/her-here is all my info.

I-864: I make enough money to support my foreign-born spouse. He/she will never need government assistance. Here is proof.

I-693: I was examined by a USCIS appointed doctor and the results show that I do not have any contagious diseases so you can safely let me live in America with my USC spouse.

OPTIONAL FORMS

I-765: I want to work in America while my application is being processed. Here is my info.

I-131: I want to travel outside of America while my application is being processed. Here is my info and the reason and why I wish to travel.

You may find it helpful to refer to these short summaries on throughout the application process. They will help keep you focused on the big picture and make the process more clear.

Time Saving Tips, Tricks & Conventions

How to Download Forms from uscis.gov

Go to uscis.gov and Click on "FORMS" on the top left of the screen.

In order to save information entered into the form, you must first download the PDF to your computer.

Here's how:

Click on "download form." The form will open in your browser in PDF format.

Click "file" then "save page as" and specify a location where you would like it to download to.

Close the web version and open the file from your computer, enter your info, then click "save as." You can now save your entries.

If you enter info directly into the form on the website, it will not be saved – this can be very frustrating!

Benefits of Typing Entries

An advantage of using the fill-in PDF's, besides legibility, is that they will format, and spell entries for you. For example, USCIS prefers last names entered in all CAPS. Most of the fill-in forms will automatically convert your last name entries into all CAPS for you – nice! Likewise, many of the forms will format phone numbers, Social Security Numbers and Alien Numbers. Enter the number series without dashes or parentheses, and the form will add them.

Sometimes, your computer will show an error message when entering "None" in a box that usually requires a number, such as your Alien or Social Security Number. Ignore this message, because there isn't an error.

Similarly, an entry of "None" into one these boxes might be "auto-corrected" to 000-000-000. If this happens, just leave the box blank and hand write "None" after printing.

The USCIS updates their forms on occasion. Please visit the USCIS website to ensure that the forms you are working on are the most recent. You can easily verify this by looking at the little entry (e.g. Rev. 12/08/13) on the bottom right hand side of any page of any form, and at the top right of the first page of instructions.

Download and read the instructions that USCIS provides for each form. The USCIS instructions are very precise, but they often contain information that is irrelevant for many people. One purpose of this kit is to clearly present the official instructions. Nevertheless, be sure to familiarize yourself with the official instructions, because, like the forms themselves, the instructions are revised periodically. If you find a discrepancy between advice offered here and on the official USCIS instructions, follow the latter.

Tips on Completing Forms

Before you begin completing the forms, here are a few helpful tips.

Type your entries if possible

Print everything single sided

Handwrite anything that cannot be accomplished by typing

If you prefer the pen and paper route, be sure to **print in black ink pen** (do not use any other color).

Sign and date all forms as required. This sounds obvious but it is a common oversight.

4 Things to Avoid when Completing Forms

Avoid submitting originals of Birth Certificates, Marriage Certificates, Passports and other requested documents, unless specifically required. Submit clean photocopies. During your interview, you will bring the originals and the Officer will compare them to the copies.

Avoid submitting oversized or undersized attachments. Submitting odd sized documents can easily disorganize and delay the processing of your application. Try to submit everything on 8.5x11 sheets. For smaller items such as Birth Certificates and Passports, copy them onto 8.5x11 paper. For larger items, reduce them while copying. As a last resort, fold the pages to fit within the bounds of 8.5x11. The USCIS will two hole punch your application at the top and bind it together.

Avoid listing a P.O. Box as your address.

Avoid entering "n/a" (not available or not applicable) when "None" is appropriate. For example, Alien Number: "n/a" could indicate that you have an Alien Number, but that it is not available (it is lost, damaged or stolen), while "None" indicates that you do not have an Alien Number. In most cases, "None" is more accurate. This is a subtle point, but one worth considering if you want to optimize the processing of your application.

How to Include Attachments and Continuation Sheets

For our purposes, _attachments_ are documents that the USCIS requests by name, such as copies of your Birth Certificate and Passport.

Label every attachment with a title and description, even if it is obvious. For example, on the copy of your Birth Certificate, write on a blank section of the paper "Birth Certificate of [name, status and Alien Number (if any)]." For documents such as Marriage Certificates that fill an entire page, highlight the title of the document and your names.

Continuation sheets, on the other hand, are not requested by name by the USCIS but are added at your discretion to further clarify or answer a question.

Label every continuation sheet with the question that your response refers. Write your full name, status, Alien Number (if you have one), and Social Security Number (if any) on the top of the document, and then sign and date it at the bottom. If you have more than one continuation sheet, assign consecutive letter names to them.

Here is a continuation sheet template. Simply replace your information within the appropriate brackets – feel free to adapt it to your purposes.

CONTINUATION SHEET TEMPLATE

[Form]
[U.S. Citizen or Alien Name]
[Alien Number] (if any)
[Social Security Number] (if any)

Continuation Sheet [A, B, C etc.]

[Form] [Part/Section], [Question Number (and/or letter)]

[Enter complete USCIS question]

[Answer question]

[Signature and Date]

Translating Foreign Documents

USCIS requires you to submit certified translations for all foreign language documents. The translation should include a cover letter in English consisting of the certifier's name, signature, address and date of certification. Translations must be word for word. You don't have to pay for a certified translator; you can have a trustworthy friend or colleague who is fluent in both English and the language of the document being translated translate for you, or you may do it yourself. The USCIS suggests the following format:

TRANSLATOR CERTIFICATION TEMPLATE
Include in front of each translated document
···

Translator Certification

I [name] certify that I am fluent in English and [other language], and that the attached document is an accurate translation of [the foreign spouse's full name] [foreign spouse's Alien Number (if any)] [name of document].

Signature _____ Date_____

[Typed Name of Translator]
[Address]
[Phone Number]

Passport-style Photos

Many forms require the submission of "Passport style photographs." **The photos should be in color, have a white background, be glossy and be unedited. You can have the photos taken at a local photo studio or**, if you have the means, **take them yourself.**

In general, all requested "passport-style" photos should be:

Identical
In color
2x2 inches or 5x5 centimeters in size
Printed on photo-quality paper
Taken within the past 30 days
Full face, front view, with a plain white or off-white background
Between 1 inch and 1 3/8 inches from the bottom of the chin to the top of the head
Taken in normal street attire

How to Attach Photographs to Your Application

Label all photos on the backside with your name and status. For Example: Johanna ADAMS – Alien Beneficiary. One simple way of submitting photographs with your application is to place each photo in separate clear plastic bags. Staple the bags to sheets of 8.5x11 paper, label the paper with relevant info (who, when and where), and include the sheets behind the appropriate forms.

Batch Copy to Save Time

Many USCIS forms request the exact same documents as attachments. For example, the foreign spouse must send a copy of his/her Birth Certificate with forms I-130, I-485 and I-765. You can save time by photocopying all your documents at once. The chart below shows how many copies you need of each of your documents. Potentially, you can copy all your documents in one trip to the copy machine, set them aside and attach them to the appropriate forms, as needed. This will save you countless time and confusion.

List of Documents and Number of Copies Needed For Initial Filing

Document	Form	I-130	I-485	I-864	I-693	I-765	I-131	TOTAL
Birth Certificate. Foreign spouse		1	1			1		3
Birth Certificate. U.S. Citizen		1		1				2
Passport. Foreign spouse			1			1	1	3
Passport. U.S. Citizen		1		1				2
Visa (Foreign Spouse)			1					1
I-94 (Foreign Spouse)			1					1
Photo (Passport-style). Foreign spouse		1	2			2	2	7
Photo (Passport-style). U.S. Citizen		1						1
G-325A. Foreign spouse		1	1					2
G-325A. U.S. Citizen		1						1
Criminal History (if any) Foreign spouse			1					1
Death/Divorce Cert. of Previous Spouse's		1	1					2
Tax Returns U.S. Citizen				1				1
Employment Authorization Doc. (EAD) Foreign						1		1
Marriage Certificate		1	1					2
Evidence of Marriage		1						1
Vaccination and Health Records (Foreign Spouse)					1			1

★ **Note:** If any of these documents are in a language other than English, you must submit them along with certified translations. See the previous page for more information.

Step I: Filling Forms

Step I consists of example entries and explanations for each of the forms required to get your marriage based Green Card. Use the examples entries as a guide when filling out the USCIS forms yourself. The forms are presented in the order in which they should appear when submitting your application. We begin with Form I-130, Petition for Alien Relative.

I-130, Petition for Alien Relative

The purpose of this form is for the U.S. citizen (or permanent resident) to establish the existence of a relationship with his/her foreign spouse who would like to immigrate to the U.S. In other words, this form tells USCIS that you are a U.S. Citizen and that you want your foreign-born spouse to live with you in America and you are providing proof of our marriage.

The USCIS updates their forms on occasion. Please visit the USCIS website to ensure that the form you are working on is the most recent. You can easily verify this by looking at the little entry (e.g. Rev. 10/08/10) on the bottom right hand side of any page of any form, and the top right of the first page of instructions (e.g. Expires 10/31/2011).

Download and read the instructions that USCIS provides. Always read the official instructions carefully, especially if your situation is complex. The instructions, like the forms themselves, are revised periodically. If you find a discrepancy between advice offered here and on the official USCIS instructions, follow the latter.

Example Entries

A. Relationship. **You (the U.S. citizen) are the petitioner. Your foreign spouse is the beneficiary.**

1. I am filling this petition for my: Check the first box "Husband/Wife"
2. Are you related by adoption? Check appropriate box
3. Did you gain permanent residence through adoption? Check appropriate box.

B. Information about you (The U.S. citizen)
(Notice that <u>this section is on the left side of the page only</u>)

1. Name   (Family name in CAPS) (First)   (Middle)
   Example: ADAMS   John   Robert
       If you are assuming your spouse's last name, indicate it here.

2. Address (Number and Street)   (Apt. No.)
   Example: 789 Oak Street (Always write out "Street," "Avenue," etc.).   33A or None

   (Town or City)   (State/Country) (Zip/Postal Code)
     New York   NY   11220

3. Place of Birth   (Town or City)   (State/County)
   Example: Brookline   MA

4. Date of Birth
   Example: 06/21/1978

5. Gender Check appropriate box

6. Marital Status Check "Married"

7. Other names used (including maiden name) Example: "None"

8. Date and Place of Present Marriage (if married) Example: 02/14/2009, Reno, NV USA

9. U.S. Social Security Number If using a computer, do not enter dashes, because the form will insert them for you. Example: 012-34-5678

10. Alien Registration Number If you are a U.S. citizen, enter "None."

11. Names of Prior Husband(s)/Wive(s) Example: Janet Bennett or "None".

12. Date(s) Marriage(s) Ended Example: 12/21/2004 or "None."

13. If you are a U.S. citizen, complete the following:
    My citizenship was acquired through (check one):
    Check the appropriate box. Most often, this is the first box –"Birth in the U.S."

If you are a lawful permanent resident alien, complete the following:
Date and place of admission for or adjustment to lawful permanent residence and class of admission.
Example: 08/02/1992 NY K-2. If you are a U.S. citizen, leave blank.

14b. Did you gain permanent resident status through marriage to a U.S. citizen or lawful permanent resident?
Check appropriate box. If you are a U.S. citizen, check "No."

C. Information about your relative (your foreign born "alien" spouse)
(Notice that this section is on the right side of the page only)

1. Name (Family name in CAPS)   (First)   (Middle)
   Example: ADAMS   Johanna   Gottlieb
   If you are assuming your spouse's last name, indicate it here.

2. Address (Number and Street) (Apt. No.)
   Example: 789 Oak Street   33A or "None"

   (Town or City)   (State/Country)   (Zip/Postal Code)
   New York   NY   11220

3. Place of Birth Example: Hamburg, Germany

4. Date of Birth Example: 12/16/1980

5. Gender Check appropriate box.

6. Marital Status Check "Married"

7. Other names used (including maiden name) Example: GOTTLIEB (maiden)

8. Date and Place of Present Marriage (if married) Example: 02/14/2009 Reno, NV USA

9. U.S. Social Security Number Example: 147-25-8369 or "None"

10. Alien Registration Number Example: 876-543-210

11. Name(s) of Prior Husband(s)/Wive(s) Example: Ditters von DITTERSDORF

12. Date Marriage(s) Ended Example: 03/16/2007

13. Has your relative ever been in the U.S.? Check "Yes"

14. If your relative is in the U.S., complete the following:
    He or She last arrived as a: (visitor, student, stowaway, without inspection, etc.)

    Enter Visa type if appropriate, such as K-1, K-3 etc.

Arrival/Departure record (I-94) Example: 212-68056805   Date arrived Example: 11/20/2009

Date authorized stay expired, or will expire, as shown on Form I-94 or I-95
Example: 11/20/2011
Some visas do not have a set expiration date stamped on the I-94. Instead, there is often a code such as D/S (duration of stay). If this is the case, enter the code in place of the date.

15. Name and Address of present employer (if any) Example: "None"
    Date this employment began Leave blank if "None."

16. Has your relative ever been under immigration proceedings?
    Check the appropriate box
    If "Yes", enter where and when. If you must check Removal, Exclusion/Deportation, Rescission or Judicial Proceedings, consider hiring an immigration attorney.

PAGE 2

C. Information about your alien relative (continued)

17. List husband/wife and all children of your relative. (Include yourself)
    Example: John Robert ADAMS   Husband   06/21/1978   USA
    This question can cause confusion. Remember that the form is being filled out by the U.S. citizen. The U.S. citizen is being asked to provide info about his/her spouse. Your spouse's spouse is you; therefore your name (the U.S. citizen's) should appear above.

18. Address in the United States where your relative (spouse) intends to live
          (Street Address)   (Town or City)   (State)
    Example: 789 Oak Street   New York   NY

19. Your relative's address abroad. (Include street, city, province and country) Phone Number (if any)
    Example: Kieler Strasse 1211 D-22543   Hamburg, Germany   31207125601

20. If your relative's native alphabet (writing system) is other than Roman letters, write his or her name and foreign address in the native alphabet (characters).
    Have your spouse enter his/her full name in his/her native language. Sometimes the fill-in PDF will not accept certain characters. In that case, print out the form and write it in by hand.

    (Name)   Address   (Include street, city, province and country):
    Example: Same   Kieler Straße 1211 D-22543   Hamburg, Germany

21. If filing for your husband/wife, give last address at which you lived together. (Include street, city, province, if any, and country):
                                          From: To:
    Example: 789 Oak Street New York, NY 11220   11/20/2009   Present

22. Complete the information below if your relative is in the United States and will apply for adjustment of status. Your relative is in the United States, and he or she will apply for adjustment of status to that of a lawful permanent resident at the USCIS office in:
Enter the city and state of the USCIS office closest to your home. Use the USCIS office locater to find out which office that is. http://tinyurl.com/officelocater
Example: New York, NY

If your relative is **not** eligible for adjustment of status, he or she will apply for a visa abroad at the American consular post in: Enter appropriate consulate or n/a.

D. Other information (about the U.S. Citizen)

1. If separate petitions are also being submitted for other relatives, give names of each and relationship.
   Example: "None"

2. Have you ever before filed a petition for this or any other alien?
   Check appropriate box
   If "Yes," give name, place and date of filing and result. If "No", leave blank.

E. Signature of petitioner.
   Sign, date and enter phone number.

F. Signature of person preparing this form, if other than the petitioner.
   Leave blank unless a lawyer helped you complete this form.

Attachments for Form I-130

Form G-1145: E-Notification of Application/Petition Acceptance
If you would like to receive an email or text message confirming the receipt of your application, complete Form G-1145: E-Notification of Application/Petition Acceptance and attach it to the front of Form I-130. You only need to submit one copy of G-1145 to receive an electronic receipt for each form you submit.

I: Documents that prove you are a U.S. Citizen

Although you are only required to include 1, you should include 2 (usually your Birth Certificate and Passport), if possible.

Primary Documents

- A copy of your Birth Certificate (front and back).

- A copy of <u>all</u> pages of your U.S. Passport. Admittedly, submitting blank Passport pages appears odd. Some people have submitted only the Passport pages with entries with success. Nevertheless, it is recommended that you submit all pages as requested

Optional or Additional Documents for proof of U.S. Citizenship or Permanent Residency

- A copy of your proof of naturalization (if applicable).

- A copy of your proof of permanent residency (if applicable).

- A copy of Form FS-240, Report of Birth Abroad of a Citizen of the U.S. issued by a U.S. Embassy or Consulate (if applicable).

- An original statement from a U.S. Consular Officer, verifying that you are a U.S. citizen with a valid Passport (if applicable).

II: Documents that Prove Family Relationship (marriage in your case)

REQUIRED

- A copy of your Marriage Certificate (never send an original; you will not get it back.)

- Documents showing any previous marriages that were terminated (if applicable).

- Color Passport-style photos of you and your spouse (1 each). The photos should have a white background, be glossy, un-retouched and not mounted. The suggested dimensions are 2x2 inches or 5x5 centimeters. Your face should measure about one inch from your chin to the top of your hair. Print your name and Alien Number (if any) on the back of each photo, and place in a small plastic bag. Attach the bag to an 8.5x11piece of paper. Label the paper "Passport-style Photo," plus your name and include the attachment.

- A completed and signed Form G-325A Biographic Information completed by foreign spouse. We will cover this next

- A G-325A the U.S. citizen containing only your name and signature.

III: Evidence of a Marriage in Good Faith

In addition to the required forms shown above, you should submit other evidence that demonstrates the "bona fide" good faith – i.e. your marriage was entered into out of love and not for acquiring a Green Card. It is always better to send more documentation than less when dealing with the USCIS.

One of the primary qualities that the Officer is looking for is TRUST. One of the best ways to demonstrate trust is to have shared finances. Granting someone access to your bank account exhibits a high level of trust. That is why it is highly recommended that you present evidence of "comingling of financial resources." If you do not have a joint bank account, open one as soon as possible.

Examples of Evidence of a Bona Fide Marriage
Submit as many as possible

- Documents **showing that you live together**. Provide a copy of your lease or apartment contract with both of your names and signatures and copies of utility/service bills.

- Proof of **joint ownership of property**, such as a copy of your mortgage or lease.

- **Birth Certificate(s) of child(ren)** born to you and your spouse.

- Documentation showing **"co-mingling of financial resources."** This includes canceled checks from joint bank account, joint bank statements, joint credit card bills, joint investments, jointly filed tax returns, etc.

- Evidence of **joint insurance** such as car, health, dental, life etc.

- **Photographs of you and your spouse together**. Photos showing both you and your spouse with other family members or photos taken during your wedding ceremony are particularly helpful. USCIS prefers "original" photographs, not photocopies. Be sure to include the name of everyone in the photos, the date the photo was taken and the location.

  One way to include photos in your application is to have your digital photos printed (or print them yourself on photo paper), and then staple them to 8.5x11 paper and provide names, dates, and locations around the photo with a pen. This makes it easier for USCIS to bind your entire application into single document without photos floating around.

- **Affidavits sworn to by a U.S. citizen**, not you or your spouse, and preferably not anyone in your immediate family, but a close friend, mentor, advisor, colleague, professor, etc. Make sure the affidavits include the full name, address, date and place of birth, relation to you, and a complete explanation with details of how the person writing the Affidavit acquired their knowledge of your marriage. Basically your colleague is taking an oath that they have personal knowledge or the "bona fides" (good faith) of your marriage i.e. you marriage was entered into out of love rather than an attempt to get Green Card. Remember you need two of these. You can send three if proof of marriage is lacking but don't send more than three. See the template below for help with creating Sworn Affidavits.

  ★ **Tip:** Include pictures of you and your spouse with the person filling an Affidavit. As with all photographs, be sure to indicate names, dates and locations. This is not required but is helpful to the officers examining your case for establishing the identity of the person who submits an Affidavit.

SWORN AFFIDAVIT FOR FROM I-130 (& I-751) TEMPLATE

BEFORE THE UNITED STATES CITIZENSHIP & IMMIGRATION SERVICES
UNITED STATES DEPARTMENT OF HOMELAND SECURITY

Affidavit of [Name of Author] on the Bona Fides of the Marriage of
[Foreign Spouse's Name, Alien Number] and
U.S. Citizen [Name]

To Whom It May Concern,

My name is [...] I live at [...]. I was born in [...] on [...]. I am a [title] at [organization,]. This is written regarding my observation that [...] and [...] live happily together as husband and wife. I have been [name's] [relationship] since [date]. I have spent time with [names'] wife/husband, [name], on numerous occasions, particularly [when or where]. I can attest that they are not only married, but that they have a sound and stable marriage.

Please feel free to contact me if I can be of further assistance in this matter.

Thank you for your consideration.

Sincerely,

[Signature] [Date]
[Typed name]
[Address]
[Phone number]

- Any other relevant documentation to establish that you are married. This can include items such as mail addressed to both of you, utility or service bills, copies of plane tickets/boarding passes showing a trip you took together, wedding invitations, joint ownership of any property, such as a vehicle, joint memberships to any clubs, gyms or wholesale centers, etc.

The above list includes examples of the types of documentation that USCIS would like to see. You do not need to have everything listed above, and you may include forms of evidence that are not mentioned. Use your judgment. To accelerate the approval of your application, **send as many relevant forms of documentation possible**. It is better to overwhelm them with evidence of your "bona fide" marriage, than to delay your application by receiving a request for more information.

IV: Payment

Currently, the fee for Form I-130 is **$420.00**. This fee increases occasionally, and, although this kit is updated, it is wise to double check that the fee is correct before you submit your application.

You may include a money order or a personal check from a U.S. bank. A check is recommended, as you will have a record of when it was cashed and, therefore, you can gauge the progress of your application.

Make the check or money order out to U.S. Department of Homeland Security (do not abbreviate) and write the name of the form on the memo line.

If you need additional room to explain your case, attach a continuation sheet.

You do not need to include a cover letter for each individual form. Instead, create a cover letter for your entire submission.

Now that you're done with Form I-130, set it aside. We will cover assembling and mailing instructions after all of the forms are completed.

Next on the list is Form G-325A.

G-325A, Biographic Information

The purpose of this form is to provide basic biographic information to the USCIS. The foreign spouse must complete the form, while the U.S. spouse only needs to enter his/her name and signature. This is because the biographic information of the U.S. spouse is contained on form I-130 and need not be repeated. However, this rule has changed in the past and may change again, it is recommended that you complete the form it its entirety just to be safe.

For the foreign spouse, the G-325A is required as an attachment to both the I-130 and I-485. He or she can save time by typing entries into the fill-in PDF and printing out multiple copies. The U.S. spouse needs only one copy to include as an attachment to Form I-130.

Double Check that you have Form G-325**A** not (not the plain G-325 or the G-325**B** or **C**).

The USCIS updates their forms on occasion. Please visit the USCIS website to ensure that the form you are working on is the most recent. You can easily verify this by looking at the little entry (e.g. Rev. 10/08/10) on the bottom right hand side of any page of any form, and the top right of the first page of instructions (e.g. Expires 10/31/2011).

Download and read the instructions that USCIS provides. Always read the official instructions carefully, especially if your situation is complex. The instructions, like the forms themselves, are revised periodically. If you find a discrepancy between advice offered here and on the official USCIS instructions, follow the latter.

Example Entries
for Form G-325A for the <u>Foreign</u> spouse

Information about you

(Family Name) Last name in CAPS, Example: ADAMS

(First Name) Example: Johanna

(Middle Name) Example: Gottlieb

Check "Male" or "Female"

Date of Birth (mm/dd/yyyy) Example: 12/16/1980

Citizenship/Nationality Example: Germany

File Number (Alien Number) Example: 876-543-210 or "None"

All Other Names Used (Including names by previous marriages) (or maiden name) Example: GOTTLIEB –maiden, or DITTERSDORF –prior marriage

City and Country of Birth. Example: Hamburg, Germany

U.S. Social Security # (If any) Example: "None" or 147-25-8369

Information about your parents

      Family Name
Father. Example: Gottlieb
Mother (Maiden Name) Example: Schumann

      First Name
Father Example: Karl
Mother Example: Clara

      Date of Birth
Father Example: 08/04/1951
Mother Example: 01/12/1954

      City and Country of Birth (if known)
Father Example: Hamburg, Germany
Mother Example: Hamburg, Germany

      City and Country of Residence
Father Example: Hamburg, Germany
Mother Example: Hamburg, Germany

Information about your spouse

Current Husband or Wife (if none, so state)

Family Name (For wife, give maiden name) Example: ADAMS

First Name Example: John

Date of Birth (mm/dd/yyyy) Example: 06/21/1978

City and Country of Birth Example: Brookline, USA

Date of Marriage Example: 02/14/2009

Place of Marriage Example: Reno, NV

Information about your former spouses (if any)

Former husbands or Wives (If none, so state)

G-325A

Family Name (For wife, give maiden name)   First Name   Date of Birth
Example: "None" or DITTERSDORF   Ditters   11/02/1979

Date and Place of Marriage   Date and Place of Termination
Example: 04/11/2000   Germany   03/16/2007 Germany

Alternatively, if no prior spouses, enter "None" in the name box and leave the other boxes blank.

Applicant's residence last five years. List present address first.

Do not leave any time gaps in your entries. As requested, list your addresses chronologically. Start with your current address and work backwards.

Example: 789 Oak Street   New York   NY   USA   11 2009 to Present Time

If you have had more than six addresses in the past five years, make a note that you have included a continuation sheet. Attach the sheet to the back of the form detailing your situation. As with all continuation sheets, include the name/number of the form, the question to which your response refers, your full name, Alien Number (if any), signature and date.

Applicant's last address outside the United States of more than 1 year.
Example: Kieler Straße 1211 D-22543   Hamburg, Germany   From: 05 1984 to: 11 2009

Applicant's employment last five years. (If none, so state). List present employment first.

Full Name and Address of Employer

Do not leave any time gaps in your entries. As with your addresses above, list your employment history chronologically, starting with your current job and working backwards.

If you are unemployed or a student, simply enter "Unemployed" or "Student" in the first box with the appropriate dates.

If you have had more than six jobs in the past five years, make a note that you have included a continuation sheet. Attach a corresponding continuation sheet to the back of the form detailing your situation. As with all continuation sheets, include the name/number of the form, the question to which your response refers, your full name, Alien Number (if any), signature and date.

Last occupation abroad if not shown above. (Include all information requested above.)
Example: "None"

This form is submitted in connection with an application for:

Check "Status as Permanent Resident."

Sign and date the form

If your native alphabet (writing system) is other than Roman letters, write your name in your native alphabet (characters) below:

If your name usually includes Roman letters or diacritical marks that you drop when translating into English, include that here as well.
Example: English version – Schoenberg from the German "Schönberg"

Applicant: Print your name and Alien Registration Number in the box outlined by heavy border below. Enter your basic biographic info in the bold box below and you are finished.

★ **Reminder:** The foreign spouse must submit one copy of <u>G-325A with both Form I-130 AND with I-485</u>. The U.S. citizen only needs to include one copy with Form I-130.

I-485: Application to Register Permanent Residence or Adjust Status

The purpose of Form I-485 is to adjust your (the foreign spouse's) status to that of a permanent U.S. resident. Along with Form I-130, it is the most significant form of the bunch.

> The USCIS updates their forms on occasion. Please visit the USCIS website to ensure that the form you are working on is the most recent. You can easily verify this by looking at the little entry (e.g. Rev. 10/08/10) on the bottom right hand side of any page of any form, and the top right of the first page of instructions (e.g. Expires 10/31/2011).
>
> **Download and read** the instructions that USCIS provides. Always read the official instructions carefully, especially if your situation is complex. The instructions, like the forms themselves, are revised periodically. If you find a discrepancy between advice offered here and on the official USCIS instructions, follow the latter.

Example Entries

Part 1. Information about You (the foreign spouse)

Family Name *(Last Name)* Use CAPS. If you are assuming your spouse's last name, indicate it here.
Example: ADAMS

Given Name *(First Name)* Example: Johanna

Middle Name. Example: Gottlieb

Address – Street Number and Name.	Apt. #
789 Oak Street	33A

C/O *(in care of)*:	City	State	Zip Code
Enter a name or leave blank	Example: New York	NY	11220

Date of Birth: *(mm/dd/yyyy)* Example: 12/16/1980

Country of Birth Example: Germany

Country of Citizenship/Nationality Example: Germany

U.S. Social Security # Example: 147-25-8369 or "None". Allow the PDF to enter the dashes for you.

A # (Alien Registration Number) Example: 876-543-210

Date of Last Arrival *(mm/dd/yyyy)* Example: 11/20/2009

I-94 # You will find this number in your Passport on a small, attached white card.
Example: 212680568 05
If you are Canadian, and were not issued an I-94 card, enter "Canadian Visitor".

Current USCIS Status
Enter the status code that was stamped on your I-94 Card in your Passport
Example: K-3

Expires on (mm/dd/yyyy)
Enter the date of expiration displayed on your I-94 card. Example: 11/20/2011
Some visas do not have a set expiration date stamped on the I-94. Instead, there is often a code such as D/S (duration of stay). If this is the case, enter the code instead of a date.

Part 2. Application Type (Check one)

I am applying for an adjustment to permanent resident status because:

Check box A if you are seeking to become a permanent resident based on marriage to a U.S. citizen.
Leave the remainder of Part 2 blank.

Check box C if you entered the U.S. on a K-1 visa and married your spouse within 90 days

Part 3. Processing Information

A. City/Town/Village of Birth   Current Occupation
Example: Hamburg   Oboist

Your Mother's First Name   Your Father's First Name
Example: Clara   Example: Karl

Give your name exactly as it appears on your Form I-94 Arrival-Departure Record
Example: Johanna GOTTLIEB

Place of Last Entry Into the United States *(City/State)*
Example: New York, NY

In what status did you last enter? *(Visitor, student, exchange visitor, crewmember, temporary worker, without inspection, etc.)* Example: K-3

Were you inspected by a U.S. Immigration Officer? **Example: Check "Yes".**

Nonimmigrant Visa Number
This is the number on your visa in **RED INK**. It is often eight digits long and is located toward the bottom right of the page. Sometimes it may contain a letter such as C. Include the letter in your entry. Example: 12345678

★ **NOTE:** this is **not** the "control number."

Consulate Where Visa Was Issued. Example: Hamburg, Germany

Date Visa Issued *(mm/dd/yyyy)* Example: 11/01/2009

Gender Check appropriate box.

Marital Status Example: Check Married

Have you ever before applied for permanent resident status in the U.S.?
Check appropriate box.
If "Yes" give date and place of filing and final disposition

B. List your present spouse and all of your children (include adult sons and daughters). (If you have none, write "None." If additional space is needed, attach a continuation sheet to the back of this form. As with all continuation sheets, include the name/number of the form and the question to which your response refers, your full name, Alien Number (if any), signature and date.

Family Name *(Last Name)*	Given Name *(First Name)*	Middle Initial	Date of Birth *(mm/dd/yyyy)*
Example: ADAMS	John	R	06/21/1978

Country of Birth
Example: USA

A # (Alien Number) *(if any)* Example: "None." The fill-in PDF will often change "None" into 000-000-000. If this occurs, write in "None" by hand after printing.

Applying with You (for permanent residency?) Check "No"

Add biographic information on any children you might have.

Part 3. Processing Information *(Continued)*

C. List your present and past membership in or affiliation with every organization, association, fund, foundation, party, club, society . . .

This section helps USCIS root out members of groups that may pose a threat to the U.S. Most people simply enter "None." However, do not lie. If the USCIS uncovers the truth, they can impose severe penalties. Therefore, if you have affiliations with any groups that the USCIS views as threat, it is best to indicate it here and attach an explanation and consider hiring a lawyer to plead your case. On the other hand, feel free to enter any affiliations of which you are particularly proud.

Questions (Check "Yes" or "No")

If you must answer "Yes" to any one of these questions, explain on a separate piece of paper. Answering "Yes" does not necessarily mean that you are not entitled to adjust your status or register for permanent residence, although it may complicate the process. Affirmative answers to questions 15 through 18 will usually not reflect as negatively on your application as affirmative answers to any of the other questions. In all cases, provide a detailed explanation and documentation. If additional space is needed, attach a continuation sheet to the back of this form. As with all continuation sheets, include the name/number of the form and the question to which your response refers, your full name, Alien Number (if any), signature and date.

Part 4. Accommodation for Individuals With Disabilities and/or Impairments

If you have any physical handicaps, check the appropriate box and provide details below or on a continuation sheet.

Part 5. Signature

Read the fine print about your requirements to register with the USCIS and the Selective Service, then turn to the signature page.

Applicant's Statement *(Check one)*

Check the first box if you read and understood the form in English by yourself.

Check the second box if someone translated the form for you into a language in which you are fluent. If this is the case, have your translator fill out the Interpreter's Statement and Signature.

Sign, then print your name. Enter the current date your telephone number.

Part 6. Signature of Person Preparing Form, If Other Than Above

Leave blank unless someone (such as a lawyer) helped you complete this form.

Attachments to Form I-485, "Initial Evidence"

Documents

1. A copy of the foreign spouse's Birth Certificate. Provide an English translation if the Birth Certificate is in any language other than English

2. A copy of the foreign spouse's Passport. Include all pages that contain entries

3. A copy of your Marriage Certificate

4. Two identical Passport-style photos of the foreign spouse. Write full name and Alien Number on the back. Drop photos into clear plastic bags and attach them to sheets of paper. Label the paper with the same info.

5. A copy of the foreign spouse's I-94 (front and back) (this is in your Passport)

6. A copy of the foreign spouse's Visa (this is in your Passport)

7. Criminal History. If you have ever been arrested, spent time in prison, rehabilitation, or had a criminal record that was erased, submit documentation. You do not need to submit documentation for traffic violations unless they involved drugs, alcohol, arrest points on your driver's license, or a fine of more than $500.

8. Documentation of termination of previous marriages (Divorce or Death Certificate) (if any)

Forms to attach to I-485

<u>Required</u>

G-325A, Biographic Information. (foreign spouses only)

I-864, Affidavit of Support

I-693, Medical Examination of Aliens Seeking Adjustment of Status

<u>Optional</u>

I-765, Application for Employment Authorization, if you want to work while your application is processed (optional)

I-131, Application for Travel Document, if you need to travel outside the United States while your application is processed (optional)

Payment

Currently the total fee for form I-485 is **$1070** ($985 + $85 for the Biometrics – fingerprinting and photos).This fee increases occasionally, and although this kit is updated, it is wise to double check that the fee is correct. You may include a money order or a personal check from a U.S. bank. A check is recommended, since you will have a record of when it was cashed and, therefore, you will be able gauge the progress of your application. Make the check out to U.S. Department of Homeland Security (do not abbreviate), and write the name of the form on the memo line.

That completes Form I-485. We will cover assembling and mailing instructions after all the forms have been filled.

Onto Form I-864.

I-864: Affidavit of Support

The U.S. citizen spouse files this form to prove that he or she has adequate financial resources to support his or her foreign spouse. You need to prove that your income is 25% over the poverty level.

The poverty level for 2013 for two people is $15,510, so you must show evidence that your income is over $19,387.00. If you are currently in the military you are only required to sponsor at 100 percent of the poverty level. You must include proof of active military service.

You can check here for annual updates to the poverty line at http://tinyurl.com/federalpovertyline

If your income is comfortably over the current poverty line, skip ahead to the example entries.

If you cannot meet the income requirements:

> You can include your assets or those of any household member*
> (they must complete Form I-864A).

> You can include income from any household relative as a co-sponsor
> (they must complete Form I-864A).

> You can include income from your foreign spouse, if the income will continue coming from the same source after he or she obtains a permanent residence. (Form I-864A is not needed).

> You can include the help of someone not in your household as a joint sponsor
> (they must complete Form I-864 **NOT I-864A**).

*If you choose to **include your assets** to enhance your resources, keep in mind that they must be **at least three times** the difference between the annual income and the needed 125% of the poverty level. This is because the Affidavit is in effect for three years. For example, if you need $18,000 in income (to be 25% over the poverty line), and had an annual income of $15,000, you would need an extra $3,000 in assets for three years, meaning a total of $9,000 in assets in addition to your income. Another issue with assets is that they must be able to be converted into cash within one year without "undue hardship."

If your yearly income is lacking and your assets are marginal, get a **co-sponsor or Joint sponsor**. If you do not have a job or a steady income from other sources (such as retirement income), you will likely have to get a sponsor even if your assets are adequate. If your situation is complex, consider hiring an attorney.

Receiving government assistance (welfare, or "means-tested public benefits") does not disqualify anyone from being a sponsor. However, you cannot count your government benefits as income. In rare cases, the USCIS can deny your affidavit based on the likelihood of the foreign spouse becoming a financial burden to the U.S government. Again, if your situation is complex, consider hiring an attorney.

★ **Tip:** If you are sponsoring more than one immigrant (your spouse and child for example), you can fill out this form once and then make a photocopy to send. You do not need to fill out this form twice. Likewise, you do not need to include duplicates of supporting financial documents (tax returns, etc.) if you are sponsoring more than one immigrant, one copy is enough.

★ **NOTE:** Previous versions of this form required notarization. Fortunately, this is no longer the case.
★ However, <u>Form I-864**A** *does* require notarization.</u>

The USCIS updates their forms on occasion. Please visit the USCIS website to ensure that the form you are working on is the most recent. You can easily verify this by looking at the little entry (e.g. Rev. 10/08/10) on the bottom right hand side of any page of any form, and the top right of the first page of instructions (e.g. Expires 10/31/2011).

Download and read the instructions that USCIS provides. Always read the official instructions carefully, especially if your situation is complex. The instructions, like the forms themselves, are revised periodically. If you find a discrepancy between advice offered here and on the official USCIS instructions, follow the latter.

Example Entries

Part 1. Basis for filing Affidavit of Support.

1. I, [your name] (Example: John Robert ADAMS) am the sponsor submitting this affidavit of support because (Check only one box):

   Check box a if you are the Petitioner and you are filing for the immigration of your (relative) spouse. Leave remainder of Part I blank.

   If you are the Joint Sponsor, **Check box** d.

Part 2. Information on the principle immigrant. (your foreign spouse)

2. Last Name   Example: ADAMS
   First Name   Middle Name
   Johanna   Gottlieb

3. Mailing Address Street Number and Name *(Include Apartment Number)*
   Example: 789 Oak Street, Apt. 33A

City	State/Province	Zip/Postal Code	Country
Example: New York,	NY	11220	USA

4. Country of Citizenship Example: Germany

5. Date of Birth *(mm/dd/yyyy)* Example: 12/16/1980

6. Alien Registration Number *(if any)* Example: 876-543-210 or "None."

7. U.S. Social Security Number *(if any)* Example: 147-25-8369 or "None."

Part 3. Information on the Immigrant(s) you are sponsoring.

8. Check the box "I am sponsoring the principal immigrant named in Part 2 above."
   Check "Yes"

9. Check box 9 only if you are sponsoring your children or other relative within six months of filing this application. In most cases, leave a-e blank.

10. Enter the total number of immigrants you are sponsoring on this form from **Part 3**, Items **8** and **9**.
    Example: Enter 01 in the boxes if you are only sponsoring your spouse.
    Example: Enter 02 if you are sponsoring your spouse and your child.
    Example: Enter 03 if you are sponsoring your spouse, and your two children, etc.

Part 4. Information on the Sponsor (the U.S. citizen)

Fill in your basic biographical information.

11. Name
    Last Name
    Example: ADAMS
    First Name   Middle Name
    Example: John   Robert

12. Mailing Address
    Street Number and Name *(Include Apartment Number)*
    Example: 789 Oak Street, Apt. 33A
    City   State or Province
    Example: New York   NY
    Country   Zip/Postal Code
    Example: USA   11220

13. Place of Residence *(if different from mailing address)*
    Enter address if different, If not; enter "SAME" in the first box.

14. Telephone Number *(Include Area Code or Country and City Codes)*
Example: (212) 555-2591

15. Country of Domicile
Example: USA

16. Date of Birth *(mm/dd/yyyy)*
Example: 06/21/1978

17. Place of Birth *(City)* State or Province Country
Example: Brookline MA USA

18. U.S. Social Security Number *(Required)*
Example: 012-34-5678

19. Citizenship/Residency
Check the appropriate box. (likely the first "I am a U.S. Citizen")

20. Military Service *(To be completed by petitioner sponsors only)*
Check appropriate box

Part 5. Sponsor's **household size.**

This section can cause confusion. The key is not counting anyone twice.

21. Your Household Size - <u>DO NOT COUNT ANYONE TWICE</u>

Persons you are sponsoring in this affidavit:

a. Enter the number you entered on line 10 (on the first page of this document)
Enter 0 1 for your spouse
Enter 0 2 for your spouse and your child
Example: Enter 03 if you are sponsoring your spouse, and your two children, etc.

Persons NOT sponsored in this affidavit:

b. Yourself (1 is already entered for you).

c. If you are currently married, enter "1" for your spouse.
Enter 0 because you **are sponsoring** your spouse.

d. If you (the U.S. citizen) have dependent children, enter the number. If **not, enter zero.**

e. If you have any other dependents, enter the number. If **not, enter zero.**

f. If you have sponsored anyone else with this form who are now permanent residents, enter the number here. If not, enter zero.

g. **OPTIONAL:** If you have <u>siblings, parents, or adult children</u> that live with you, and who are combining their income with yours **(only if yours is insufficient)** by submitting Form I-864A, enter the number here. **If not, enter zero.**

h. Add together lines and enter the number here. **Household Size:**

Example: You and your foreign spouse =02
Example: You, your foreign spouse plus your child =03
Example: You your foreign spouse, your child and your father (who is helping you sponsor your spouse) =04

Part 6. Sponsor's income and employment.

In Part 6, the USCIS verifies that you can financially support your foreign-born spouse in America, so that he or she will not become a financial burden to the government. As long as you show that you are comfortably over (25% above) the poverty line, your chances of success are high. The poverty level for 2013 for two people is $15,510, so you must show evidence that your income is over $19,387.00.
http://tinyurl.com/federalpovertyline

22. I am currently: (This is still info about the U.S. citizen)

    Check appropriate box and enter requested info.
    Example: **a.** Employed as a Plumber

    Name of Employer #1 *(if applicable)*
    Example: Top Quality Heating and Cooling

    Enter more employers if needed.

23. **My current *individual* annual income:**
    Example: Example: $39,000 as shown on your Federal Tax Return which you will attach later.

24. **My current annual *household* income:**

    a. List your income from line 23 of this form.
    Re-enter your income from line 23 above. Example: $39,000

    b. Income you are using from any other person (optional) who was counted in your household size, including, in certain conditions, the intending immigrant. (See step-by-step instructions). Please indicate name, relationship and income.

c. Total Household Income: Example: $39,000
(Total all lines from 24a and 24b. Will be Compared to Poverty Guidelines –
See Form I-864P).

d. The persons listed above have completed Form I-864A. I am filing along with this form all necessary Forms I-864A completed by these persons.
Check box d. if applicable.

e. The person listed above,_____does not need to complete Form I-864 because he/she is the intending immigrant and has no accompanying dependents.
If your spouse is using her income to help you qualify and does not have any children who are applying for permanent residency with him/her, enter his/her name and check box e.

25. **Federal income tax return information.**

Check the first box if appropriate, then fill in your income for the past three years.

(Optional) I have attached photocopies or transcripts of my Federal tax returns for my second and third most recent years. Although this is optional it is highly recommended.

Part 7 only needs to be completed if your household income is at or below the poverty line. If your income exceeds the poverty line, leave this entire part blank and skip to Part 8.

Part 7. Use of assets to supplement income. *(Optional)*

If you cannot meet the income requirements you can include your assets, or those of any household member. They must complete Form I-864A.

26. **Your assets** *(Optional)*

a. Enter the balance of all savings and checking accounts. **Example: $1,800.00**

b. Enter the net cash value of real-estate holding. (Net means current assessed value minus mortgage debt.) **Example: 8,000.00**

c. Enter the net cash values of all stocks, bonds, certificates of deposit, and any other assets not already included in lines 26 (a) or (b). **Example: $5,200.00.**

d. Add together lines 26 a, b and c, and enter the number **(the total)** here. **Example: $15,000.**

27. **Your household member's assets from Form I-864A.** *(Optional)*

Assets from Form I-864A, line 12d for -

- Name of Relative_____$_____

Enter the name of your relative who is including their assets and the worth of the assets as shown on Form I-864A

28. Assets of the principal sponsored immigrant *(Optional)*

The principal sponsored immigrant is the person listed in line 2 **(your spouse).**

        a. Enter the balance of the sponsored immigrant's savings and checking accounts.
Example: $5,000.00

        b. Enter the net cash value of all the sponsored immigrant's real estate holdings.
(Net means investment value minus mortgage debt.)
Example: $0.00

        c. Enter the current cash value of the sponsored immigrant's stocks, bonds, certificates of deposit, and other assets not included on line a or b.
Example: $0.00

        d. Add together lines 28a, b, and c, and enter the number here.
Example: $5,000.00

29. Total value of assets.

Add together lines 26d, 27 and 28d and enter the number here
TOTAL: Example: 20,000.00

Part 8. Sponsor's Contract. (Between you and the Government)

This lengthy contract details the ramifications of signing and not signing the I-864 Affidavit of Support. Read it through then print your full name at 30, then sign and date at 31.

Part 9. Information on Preparer, if prepared by someone other than the sponsor.

Leave blank unless someone (such as a lawyer) helped you complete this form.

Attachments for form I-864

- Federal Income Tax returns for the most recent year are required. Returns for <u>the most three recent years are recommended</u>, including W-2s. Include a copy of every Form 1099, Schedule, or any other evidence of income if applicable. Alternatively, include evidence describing why you were not required to file. Photocopies are acceptable. If you are self-employed, include a copy of your Schedule C, D, E, or F from your most recent Federal Tax Return that establishes income from your business.

- Pay Stubs for the most recent 6 months (optional, but highly recommended).

- A letter from your employer (preferably on company letterhead), signed by your boss, stating your name, salary, how long you have been employed at the company, your job title, date employment began, and salary. You can create this letter yourself, then have your boss sign and date it. Here is template:

EMPLOYER LETTER FOR FROM I-864 TEMPLATE
Printed on employer letterhead
....

To whom it may concern,

[First Name, last name] has been employed full-time with the ABC Company since [yyyy] as a [Job Title], and is an employee in good standing with an annual salary of $[....].

Signed,

[Employer's Name], [Title]
[Company Name]
[Address]
[Phone Number]

Optional or If Applicable Attachments

If you are using the <u>income</u> of someone in your household to help qualify, include:

a. Form I-864A for each person whose income you will use. If you are using your foreign spouse's income, he or she only needs to complete the I-864A if his/her children are immigrating with him or her.

b. Proof of residency in your household and relationship to you (if they are not the intended immigrants or are not listed as dependents on your most recent tax return.)

c. If you're using your spouse's income, provide proof that his or her employment will continue from the same source after obtaining a Green Card.

d. Federal Tax Returns from the most recent year (including W-2s and 1099s) of the person who is helping you. You may include the three most recent years, if you believe this will help you qualify. Alternatively, submit evidence that they were not required to file a return.

If you are using the <u>assets</u> of someone in your household to help qualify, include:

Form I-864A for each person, **except your spouse**, whose assets you will use. Documentation about the assets—location ownership, date of acquisition and value and evidence of any liens or liabilities against these assets.

★ **Reminder:** All Forms I-864A need notarization. Many banks will notarize documents for free. You can also bring them to a local notary public and pay a small fee.

If you are using a joint sponsor or substitute sponsor, they must complete form I-864 along with the U.S. Spouse. They must also include all of the attachments that the U.S. citizen must include, such as proof of citizenship, income tax forms, pay stubs, employer letter, etc.

★ **Reminder:** If you are sponsoring more than one immigrant (your spouse and child, for example), you can fill out this form once and then make a photocopy. You do not need to fill out this form twice. Likewise, you do not need to include duplicates of supporting documents (tax returns, etc.) if you are sponsoring more than one immigrant, one copy is enough.

I-693: Report of Medical Examination and Vaccination Record

Instructions

The USCIS requires a medical exam as part of your application. The purpose of the exam is to determine if you have certain diseases. You should submit the results of the examination along with your complete application.

This form should be completed by the foreign (alien) spouse only.

You only need to fill out Part 1 of this form; the other parts will be completed by the doctor.

The doctor you visit must be approved by the USCIS as a "Designated Civil Surgeon." You can find a qualified doctor, by calling the USCIS at 1-800-375-5283 and following the automated menu (Spanish is available). You can also use the USCIS's doctor locater at: http://tinyurl.com/doctorlocator

After your examination, make sure the doctor gives you the completed Form I-693 in a sealed envelope. **Do not open it or break the seal**; the USCIS will reject it. Save the sealed envelope and include it as an attachment to Form I-485.

At the end of Part I of the form (I-693), you are asked to provide your signature. Do NOT sign this until your doctor tells you to as it must be signed in his or her presence.

Although, the filing fee for this form is included with that of Form I-485, you will have to pay the doctor for the exam.

What to Bring to your Appointment

Bring Government issued photo ID such as your Passport as well as your health records. Bring as much documentation of your vaccination history as possible. This way, you won't be burdened with receiving and paying for redundant vaccinations.

The USCIS updates their forms on occasion. Please visit the USCIS website to ensure that the form you are working on is the most recent. You can easily verify this by looking at the little entry (e.g. Rev. 10/08/10) on the bottom right hand side of any page of any form, and the top right of the first page of instructions (e.g. Expires 10/31/2011).

Download and read the instructions that USCIS provides. Always read the official instructions carefully, especially if your situation is complex. The instructions, like the forms themselves, are revised periodically. If you find a discrepancy between advice offered here and on the official USCIS instructions, follow the latter.

Example Entries

Part 1. Information About You *(The person requesting a medical exam or vaccinations must complete this part* –the foreign spouse)

Family Name (Last Name)
Example: ADAMS

Given Name (First Name)
Johanna

Full Middle Name
Gottlieb

Home Address:
Street Number and Name.
Example: 789 Oak Street

Apt. Number
Apt. 33A

Gender
Check appropriate box.

City
Example: New York

State
NY

Zip Code
11220

Phone # *(Include Area Code)* no dashes or ( )
2125552591

Date of Birth *(mm/dd/yyyy)* Example: 12/16/1980

Place of Birth *(City/Town/Village)* Example: Hamburg

Country of Birth. Example: Germany

A-Number (Alien Registration Number) *(if any)* *Example*: 876-543-210

U.S. Social Security # *(if any)* Example: 147-258-369 or "None"

★ **Remember**: do not sign this form until told to do so by the doctor. The remaining parts of this form will be completed by your doctor during or after your medical exam. Then, you'll sign the form in the doctor's presence. The doctor will seal the completed form in an envelope, and return it to you.

Congratulations! You have finished all of the required forms for your application! There are, however, a few more optional forms. One of them is the Application for Employment Authorization, which you need to complete if you (the foreign spouse) would like to work in the U.S. while your application is being processed. This is recommended because it will provide you with a convenient form of photo ID, it is free, and you will receive it quickly (1-3 months). The other optional form is the Application for Travel Document, which the foreign spouse only needs to complete if he/she plans to travel outside the United States and re-enter while the application is being processed.

I-765, Application for Employment Authorization
(optional)

Completing this form is optional. Only the foreign spouse needs to complete it if he or she would like to work while the permanent residence application is being processed.

Filing for employment authorization is recommended because, in addition to allowing you to work, it is free to file, it will provide you with a convenient form of photo ID, and you will receive it rather quickly (1-3 months).

Filling out the form is simple. You only need to fill out basic biographical information as we have done previously.

> The USCIS updates their forms on occasion. Please visit the USCIS website to ensure that the form you are working on is the most recent. You can easily verify this by looking at the little entry (e.g. Rev. 10/08/10) on the bottom right hand side of any page of any form, and the top right of the first page of instructions (e.g. Expires 10/31/2011).
>
> **Download and read** the instructions that USCIS provides. Always read the official instructions carefully, especially if your situation is complex. The instructions, like the forms themselves, are revised periodically. If you find a discrepancy between advice offered here and on the official USCIS instructions, follow the latter.

Example Entries

I am applying for: **Check the first box** "Permission to accept employment."
If you received temporary employment authorization upon entrance, you should still check the first box, as in most cases, temporary employment cannot be renewed.

1. Name (Family Name in CAPS) (First) (Middle)
   Example: ADAMS   Johanna   Gottlieb

2. Other Names Used (include Maiden Name) **Example: GOTTLIEB**

3. Address in the United States (Number and Street) Apt. Number
   Example: 789 Oak Street   Example 33A
   (Town or City)   (State/County)   (ZIP Code)
   Example: New York   NY   11220

4. Country of Citizenship/Nationality **Example: Germany**

5. Place of Birth (Town or City)   (State/Province)   (Country)
   Example: Hamburg   Germany

6. Date of Birth (mm/dd/yyyy) Example: 12/16/1980

7. Gender. Check appropriate box

8. Marital Status. Check "Married"

9. Social Security Number (include all numbers you have ever used)(if any)
   Example: 147-258-369 or "None"

10. Alien Registration Number (A-Number) or I-94 Number (if any)
    Example: 876-543-210

11. Have you ever before applied for employment authorization for USCIS?
    If you have received Employment Authorization before through another visa such as H-1B, L-1, F-1 etc.,
    Check the "Yes" box and fill out the information at the top of the next column;
    otherwise, Check "No."

12. Date of Last Entry into the U.S. (mm/dd/yyyy) Example: 11/20/2009

13. Place of Last Entry in the U.S. Example: New York

14. Manner of Last Entry. Example: K-3

15. Current Immigration Status. Example: K-3

16. Enter your eligibility code. In your case, this is ( )(C)(9) as indicated on the bottom right column of
    page 4 of the instructions for I-765 –"EAD Applicants Who Have Filed for Adjustment of Status.
    "Adjustment Applicant - (c) (9). File Form I-765 with a copy of the receipt notice or other evidence that your
    Form I-485, Application of for Permanent Residence or Adjust Status, is pending. You may file Form I-765
    together with your Form I-485." (This is what you are doing.)

17. This question does not apply to you or your spouse. Leave it blank or write "None"

Certification
Sign, then enter the date and your telephone number.

Signature of the Person Preparing Form, if other than above.
Leave blank unless someone (such as a lawyer) helped you complete this form.

Attachments for form I-765

Two identical, color Passport-style photos
Government issued photo I.D. (Passport)
A copy of your latest EAD card (front and back), if you have one.

The fee for this form is included with that of the I-485. You can double check this on the left-hand column of page eight of the USCIS instructions under "Note."

★ **Note:** If you are NOT submitting this form along with Form I-485, include a copy of the I-485 Notice of Action (I-797C) with your I-765.

Form I-131, Application for Travel Document (optional)

The foreign spouse only needs to complete this form if he or she plans to travel outside the United States, and reenter while the Adjustment of Status Application is being processed. If you do not wish file this form now, you may submit it later with a copy of the I-485 filing receipt.

> The USCIS updates their forms on occasion. Please visit the USCIS website to ensure that the form you are working on is the most recent. You can easily verify this by looking at the little entry (e.g. Rev. 10/08/10) on the bottom right hand side of any page of any form, and the top right of the first page of instructions (e.g. Expires 10/31/2011).
>
> **Download and read** the instructions that USCIS provides. Always read the official instructions carefully, especially if your situation is complex. The instructions, like the forms themselves, are revised periodically. If you find a discrepancy between advice offered here and on the official USCIS instructions, follow the latter.

Example Entries

Part 1. Information About You (the foreign spouse)

1. A Number. (Alien Registration Number) Example: 876543210

2. Date of Birth *(mm/dd/yyyy)* Example: 12/16/1980

3. Class of Admission Example: K-3

4. Gender Check appropriate box.

5. Name   (Family Name in capital letters)   (First)   (Middle)
    Example: ADAMS   Johann   Gottlieb

6. Address *(Number and Street)*   Apt. Number.
    Example: 789 Oak Street   33A
         City   State or Province   Zip/Postal Code   Country
    Example: New York   NY   11220   USA

7. Country of Birth Example: Germany

8. Country of Citizenship **Example: Germany**

9. Social Security # (if any) **Example: 147-25-8369 or "None"**

Part 2. Application Type *(Check one)*

Check box d. "I am applying for an advance parole document to allow me to return to the United States after temporary foreign travel."

Leave the remainder of Part 2 blank.

Part 3. Processing Information

1. Date of Intended Departure *(mm/dd/yyyy)* **Example: 05/15/2010**
2. Expected Length of Trip. **Example: 2 weeks.**
3. Are you, or any person included in this application, now in exclusion, deportation, removal or rescission proceedings?
   Check the appropriate box. If the answer is "Yes", consult an attorney before proceeding.

   If you are applying for an Advance Parole Document, Skip to Part 7.
   Leave questions 4. and 5. blank.

Skip to Part 7 *because you are applying for Advance Parole. Leave all intermediary parts (parts 4, 5 and 6) blank.*

Part 7. Complete Only If Applying For Advance Parole
(You are applying for Advanced Parole)

"On a separate sheet of paper, explain how you qualify for an Advance Parole and what circumstances warrant issuance of advance parole. Include copies of any documents you wish considered."

Below is a Advance Parole Letter template that you can modify to fit your purpose.

ADVANCE PAROLE LETTER TEMPLATE

U.S. Citizenship and Immigration Services
P.O. Box 805887
Chicago, IL 60680-4120

RE: I-131 Request for Advance Parole by [foreign spouse's name, Alien Number]
   Co-filing with I-485 [or, if filing separately, include I-485 filing receipt/NOA.]

Dear Sir or Madam,

I respectfully request a multiple entry Advance Parole to allow me to re-enter the U.S. after temporary foreign travel.

My U.S. citizen [husband or wife] and I would like to visit my home country to visit my parents while my application for Adjustment of Status is being approved.

Please contact me if you have any questions.

Sincerely,

[Signature] [Date]
[Typed name]
[Address]
[Phone number]

1. How many trips do you intend to use this document?
It is recommended that you check "More than one trip," since this grants you more options.

2. If the person who is intended to receive an Advance Parole Document is outside the United States, provide the location (city and country) of the U.S. Embassy or consulate of the DHS overseas office that you want us to notify.

If you plan to leave the U.S. before receiving written documentation, enter the city and country where you want your APD sent. **If you will wait for approval in the U.S., leave questions 2 and 3 blank.**

★ **NOTE:** You must wait for approval of this form before you can leave the U.S. However, you may leave once you are notified of approval, but without receiving written documentation. The policies regarding this matter have changed frequently in the past few years. It is wise to call USCIS to obtain the most current information.

3. If the travel document will be delivered to an overseas office, where should the notice to pick up the document be sent? Enter your overseas address if appropriate, if not, enter None.

Part 8. Signature

Sign, print your name, date and enter your telephone number.

Part 9. Signature of Person Preparing Form, if other than above

Leave blank unless someone (such as a lawyer) helped you complete this form.

★ **NOTE:** If you are not submitting this form along with Form I-485, include a copy of the I-485 Notice of Action (I-797C) with your I-131. In addition, if filing separately, you may file I-131 online via uscis.gov http://tinyurl.com/131online

Step II: Sending it Off

S tep II covers how to assemble and mail your completed package and well as how to deal with Requests for Evidence and the Biometrics Appointment.

Assembling Tips

Write "Original Submission" on the mailing envelope and then list the forms you're enclosing. Example: I-130; I-485; I-765, etc.

Provide a cover letter for the entire package. Include your name, address, Alien Number, and a list of the forms included. This is not required but is highly recommended because it may accelerate the processing of your application and will also function as checklist for you. See the "Initial Cover Letter Template" in Part Four of this kit.

Assemble the forms in the following order:

    (G-1145) Optional
    I-130
    G-325A Alien
    G-325A U.S. Citizen

    I-485
    G-325A Alien
    I-864
    I-693
    (I-765)
    (I-131)

Make at least two copies of your entire application including money orders and/or checks. Save one for your records and another in case the USCIS requests more information or worse –loses your application.

Do not use binders, folders or staples that cannot be easily disassembled. In fact, do not bind or staple your application at all, because the USCIS will spend time undoing it anyway.

You can use ACCO fasteners to hold together your application. Two-hole punch the top of every page, and attach the fastener. Although USCIS states that they appreciate the use of ACCO fasteners on their main "Assembly Instructions" page, there are frequent reports of various USCIS branches requesting applications to be sent without them. To add to the confusion, ACCO fasteners come in many different sizes and the distance between the punched holes varies. Since everything you send will be taken apart and reorganized to their preferences, **your best bet is to use big butterfly clips to hold the entire application together.**

Butterfly clip

Add sticker tabs to the bottom (never to the sides or tops) of the appropriate pages, to identify each form and all of the attachments.

Attach required payment to the front page of Form I-130 and I-485 with a paper clip; again, it is better not to staple it.

Label every attachment with a title and description, even if it is obvious. For example, on the copy of your Birth Certificate, write on a blank section of the paper 'Birth Certificate of [name, status and Alien Number (if any)].

For documents such as Marriage Certificates that fill an entire page, highlight the title of the document and you and your spouse's names.

When **submitting photographs**, label the back of them with the names of the people in the photograph, and the date it was taken and the location. Place the photos in separate clear plastic bags and staple the bags to sheets of 8.5x11 paper. Now label the paper with the same info you wrote on the back of the photo.

Label every continuation sheet with the question to which your response refers. Write your full name, status, Alien Number (if you have one), and Social Security Number (if any) on the top of the document then sign and date it at the bottom. If you have more than one attachment, assign consecutive letter names to them.

Fees increase occasionally, and although this kit is constantly updated, it is wise to double check that the fees are correct before submitting your application at uscis.gov.

You may **include a money order or a personal check** from a U.S. bank. A check is recommended, as you will be able to gauge the progress of your application. Make the check out to U.S. Department of Homeland Security (do not abbreviate) and write the name of the form on the memo line.

If you want to receive an email or text message confirming the receipt of your application, which is highly recommended, complete **Form G-1145: E-Notification of Application/Petition Acceptance.** Attach the completed form to the front of form I-130. You will receive an electronic receipt for each form you submitted.

Mailing

Mail everything in the same envelope to the same address. Ignore other addresses listed for individual forms. They are relevant only when a form is mailed alone.

The USCIS Chicago Lockbox:
For U.S. Postal Service:

USCIS
P.O. Box 805887
Chicago, IL 60680-4120

For Express mail and courier deliveries:

USCIS
Attn: FBAS
131 South Dearborn - 3rd Floor
Chicago, IL 60603-5517

To verify that these addresses are the most recent, check the USCIS website here:
http://tinyurl.com/USCISwheretofile
Locate the box that reads "Filing Form I-130 with Form I-485."

One recommended method of mailing is a *flat-rate priority mail envelope* from USPS. Regardless of the heft of your application, the price will be the same. If you purchase the postage online, you will receive a discount and free delivery confirmation, along with the convenience of having your mailperson pick up the package. This is not a requirement. Whichever mailing service you use, be sure to include some type of tracking or confirmation service.

After Mailing

If you filed a G-1145, you will receive an email within 24 hours of the receipt of your application, confirming acceptance of each form you submitted.

One to two weeks after mailing your application, you will receive **Notices of Action (NOA) (I-797C)** from USCIS for forms I-130, I-485, and optional forms I-765 and I-131, if you submitted them. The NOA confirms the receipt of your application including payment, date received and a Receipt Number that resembles MSC-01-012-34567.

The NOA also includes a note about **Biometrics**. This is just a fancy word for fingerprints and photographs. Soon after receiving the NOAs, the USCIS will send a detailed ASC (Application Support Center) Appointment Notice about obtaining your Biometrics. This will include a date and location along with a list of documents to bring with you to the appointment.

To find out the status of your case or to sign up to receive automatic case status updates, see the "My Case Status" on the USCIS website at http://tinyurl.com/mycasestatus

If You Move after Submitting your Application

If you move anytime during or after the application process, file Form AR-11: Change of Address immediately. Since 9/11/2001, the USCIS has been very strict with this. There are reports of people being deported for not notifying the USCIS of address changes.

Dealing with a Request for Evidence

A Request for Evidence (RFE) is a formal letter from the USCIS, and it is issued when inadequate, suspicious, incorrect or dubious data is discovered in a pending application.

Some of the reasons an RFE may be issued are:

Errors on the forms
Lack of signatures
Submission of expired forms
Lack of supporting documents
Insufficient documentation to prove a "bone fide" marriage
I-693, Medical Exam conducted by unapproved doctor

In the unlikely event that you receive one of these letters, here are some tips to help you sort it out:

Request For Evidence Tips

Mail your response as quickly as possible.

Always return the entire original request for evidence with your response to the request for evidence.

Make a photocopy of the original request for evidence for your files.

The easiest way for the USCIS to locate your file is through a receipt number (provided in any communication the USCIS sends you) and your Alien Number. Always provide these numbers when communicating with the USCIS. In addition, provide your full name and date of birth. This will ensure your application is processed faster.

When adding anything new to a case in progress, submit a self-sufficient packet so that your application can be processed as received. The examiner may not have access to previously submitted documents, and having to search for them could delay your case. Remember it is better to overwhelm USCIS with documentation than to not provide enough.

If the request is complex, consider hiring an immigration attorney

Send your response to the office listed on the RFE letter.
DO NOT send your response to the Chicago Lockbox.

The Biometrics Appointment

The Biometrics Appointment Notice will request you to appear at a specified Application Support Center at a predetermined date and time.

Only the foreign spouse is required to attend. You may both attend, but, be aware that, although many USCIS branches provide waiting areas for family members, some do not. In some smaller offices, the U.S. citizen spouse may be forced to wait outside (regardless of the weather or location).

Preparing for the Appointment

Bring the Appointment Notice (not a copy)

Bring a government issued I.D., such as your Passport and/or your Driver's License

Bring your original Marriage Certificate. This is especially important if the family name on your passport and application are different.

Bring your Social Security Card (or, at least memorize the number, since you will need it to complete paperwork while at the office)

Bring your Alien Number (or at least memorize the number, since you will need it to complete paperwork while at the office)

Dress appropriately to have your picture taken

Dress appropriately for the weather, since you may have to wait outside, regardless of the conditions.

Do not bring cell phones, cameras, or any other electronics into the office. The USCIS is particularly cranky about this.

★ **Tip:** Try to keep your fingers free of abrasions before your Biometrics appointment. During the appointment, an examiner will request to see your hands – palms facing up. They are verifying that your fingers are free of significant cuts or abrasions, and are sufficiently moist. Both of these qualities help ensure accurate fingerprints. If the examiner deems either issue a problem, you could be asked to return on a later date.

Rescheduling

If there is no possible way for you to keep the appointment, reschedule as a last resort. Check the box in the middle of the Appointment Notice "Request for Rescheduling" to reschedule. Make a copy of the notice before mailing the original to the specified address. You may wait up to month to receive another appointment notice.

Another option, if you are unable to make the original appointment, is to try a "walk-in" at your local USCIS Support Center. Not all branches allow walk-ins, but some do on specific days. Often the wait time will be longer than a scheduled appointment. If attempting a walk-in, be sure to do it before your scheduled appointment. This will give you more options if you run into problems.

Another alternative is to reschedule using INFOPASS, an online USCIS support service. http://infopass.uscis.gov

Step III: The Interview

1: Prelude – Preparing for the Interview

The interview can be intimidating, and the pressure that builds leading up to the appointment can create anxiety. However, the stress of the process can be lessened with preparation, and there are simple steps you can take before the appointment, which will increase your confidence.

Increase your confidence before the interview

Study your spouse's completed G-325A. This form, as you know, contains all your essential biographic information, including your employment and residence history, birthdays, and parents' names. Make sure that you and your spouse are able to recall information on each other's forms. Make it fun; quiz one another.

Pay extra attention to details about your residence and your spouse that you may normally overlook. Besides biographic information, Officers often ask questions about your shared residence (particularly colors), and major events – weddings, honeymoons, holidays, vacations, etc. For the weeks or months leading up to the interview, try to be more mindful than usual of the details relating to these matters. Confirm that you and your spouse agree about when your first date was, or when you first talked of marriage, etc.

Organize all your documents neatly. Immigration Officers are often rushed, and they may become agitated if you repeatedly fumble around for forms when he or she requests to see them. This can make you both nervous and add tension to the air. Avoid this by arranging your documents for easy access so you can swiftly present any document requested. Organize similar documents in stacks. For example, if asked for your tax returns for the three most recent years, hand them to the Officer as a unit.

Remind yourself that since your marriage is legitimate and in "good faith," it is tremendously difficult to fail the interview. The interview is not a PhD aural examination. If your marriage is true, it does not matter if you cannot answer a particular question. Always admit when you do not know something. Not knowing is sometimes the correct response. For example, if the Officer asks you to recite your mother in law's Social Security Number and you proudly recite it, this could raise more suspicious than if you did not know.

Read the rest of this chapter about the interview process. We will cover everything from what forms to bring, what to wear, to specific interview questions and customs.

What to Bring to the Interview

You and your spouse should bring all the documents listed on your appointment notice. Sometimes, the USCIS list is vague and will request you to bring "photo identification" and "evidence of marriage." If a primary document was not submitted with your initial filing, such as a birth certificate of a recently born child, bring the original birth certificate and a copy that the officer may add to your file.

Identification. Bring Originals

Birth Certificates for you and your spouse. REQUIRED

Birth Certificates of your children. REQUIRED (IF ANY)

Social Security Cards for you and your spouse. REQUIRED

Passport of the foreign spouse, including Form I-94 (arrival record). REQUIRED
The U.S. Citizens Passport is recommend.

Employment Authorization Card (EAD) **(foreign spouse only)**

Appointment Notice and all NOA's.

Evidence of a "bona fide" marriage

These documents are roughly listed in order of strength. Bring as many items as possible. More is better than less. Bring originals of primary documents.

Marriage Certificate

Any certificates of divorce or death showing that previous marriages (if any) have been legally terminated

Proof of "cohabitation" such as copies of leases or a mortgage, rent receipts, canceled rent checks from a joint bank account, shared utility bills and anything else to show that you live together. If you live with your parents, as an au pair, or in a situation where you do not pay rent, mortgage or utility bills, create a document stating such and have it signed and dated by the appropriate person

Joint bank statements and/or canceled checks from a joint account

Income Tax Returns, (Federal, State and City) for the years that you have been married

Shared credit card accounts

Photographs showing you and your spouse together. Bring a small, but varied collection of photos spanning the time you met up until the present day. Photos of you and your spouse with your family, especially during holidays, at your wedding, honeymoon or vacations are particularly convincing.

Joint insurance policies such as health, car, dental, house, life, etc.

Written Affidavits by non-family members confirming your marriage.

Joint investment account statements (CD's, mutual funds, etc.)

Evidence of vacations or trips taken together, such as boarding passes

Screen shots of your email accounts or copies of your phone records showing your correspondence

Matching sets of keys to your residence.

Anything else that helps prove your marriage is genuine

Tips for Bringing Documents to the Interview

The Officer will not keep your original documents, but will compare them to the copies you submitted with your application. If a copy of document was not already provided with your application, make a copy ahead of time to give to the Officer. For example, if you had a child *after* you mailed your initial application, bring the original and a copy of the child's Birth Certificate.

One of the primary qualities that the Officer is looking for is TRUST. One the best ways to demonstrate trust is to have shared finances. Granting someone access to your bank account exhibits a high level of trust. That is why it is strongly recommended that you present evidence of "comingling of financial resources." If you do not have a joint bank account, open one immediately.

Organize your documents carefully for easy access, so that you can present them to the Officer in stacks. For example, if the Officer asks for evidence of a "bona fide" marriage, hand the Officer the entire stack of evidence.

When bringing photographs, label the back of them with the name of the people in the photograph, and the date it was taken. Place the photos in separate clear plastic bags and staple the bags to sheets of 8.5x11paper. Label the paper with the same info you wrote on the back of the photo.

Producing little evidence of your marriage may cause the interview to be more intense. If you and your spouse have a unique living situation (such as living in different cities) that prevents you from having many of the documents listed above, you should prepare ample explanations and documentation. For example, you can include airline itineraries, emails, exchanged cards, phone records, photos etc. If your situation is complex, consider hiring an immigration attorney to accompany you to the interview.

If the foreign spouse feels uncomfortable conversing in English during the interview, consider bringing an interpreter. Even if the U.S. spouse is able to interpret for you, the USCIS Officers usually will not allow it. The interpreter must be at least eighteen years old and be fluent in English and the foreign spouse's language.

If the alien spouse has been arrested and/or convicted of a serious crime, consider hiring an immigration attorney. If you choose to proceed without an attorney, be sure to bring copies of all relevant police and court records.

2: The Day of the Interview

In general, it is a good sign if your appointment is early in the day. USCIS often schedules simpler cases earlier in the morning, because they can go through them quickly and, therefore, avoid getting off schedule. This is not a rule, but only a general guideline. Do not be frightened if your appointment is later in the day.

Dress as if you are attending a job interview. Women should wear business-style dresses or suits. Men should wear collared and buttoned shirts (tie and jacket optional,) with slacks (no jeans).

Plan to arrive at least 30 minutes (but no more than an hour) early to your appointment. The interview will typically take place in a large government building, and you will have to pass security similar to that encountered at an airport. In most cases, you will not be allowed to bring your cell phone or any other electronic device past the security checkpoint. Once you clear security, locate the interview area; this can be challenging and intimidating in some of the larger complexes, so don't hesitate to ask for directions.

Enter the waiting room, and check-in with the receptionist as you would in a doctor's office. The receptionist will take your official appointment notice and ask you to have a seat. You may have to wait as little as 15 minutes, or as long as two hours. Use this time to go over your documents.

3: During the Interview

The Officer will enter the waiting room and summon you by your shared last name or the foreign spouse's full name. Be sure not to miss this call, because it can cause serious confusion and delay. The Officer will take you to his private office and begin the first phase of the interview process.

Phase One – Housekeeping

After entering the room, the Officer will ask you to remain standing, raise your right hand, and swear an Oath of Honesty. The Officer may or may not turn on a video camera, and you will be invited to sit down. If the Officer does not disclose his name at this point, politely ask for it and write it down. If your application is denied, the Officer's name will become a critical piece of information.

Now the Officer will begin requesting specific documents. He/she may ask for any document that was listed on the appointment notice. Often, they will focus on comparing the originals (such as such as Birth and Marriage Certificates) to the previously submitted copies, in an effort to verify their integrity. While your files are being verified, do not try to fill the silence with polite conversation. Wait patiently and do not be intimidated by the silence.

Phase Two – Questioning

After confirming your documents, the questions will begin. Many times, the questions will start with basic biographic information and progress to the more detailed. The Officer will question each of you separately. Resist the urge to answer for your spouse. Listen carefully. If you do not understand a question, ask to have it repeated. Never guess or offer information that isn't requested. Keep your responses precise and concise. If the Officer wants more details, he or she will ask you follow-up questions. Remember that the Officers have tight schedules and that they are pleased when interviews last less than 15 minutes.

The most vital information to know is your date of marriage, date of the foreign spouse's admission to the U.S., birthdays, your shared addresses and date you began living together. Keep in mind that nothing you say during any part of the interview is "off the record." If the Officer appears to be engaging in light conversation, do not let down your guard.

A good attitude is crucial. Some Officers may be ill mannered or even antagonistic. This is uncommon, but possible. If you experience this, keep your cool. Never get angry or engage in an argument. Stay calm and polite, regardless of any rudeness. Immigration Officers wield great power, and they have their "discretion" at their disposal. This means they can, theoretically, deny your application because they felt like doing so. You can appeal, but it is a precarious process and one you should avoid at all costs.

In preparation for the interview, review the following common questions listed below.

Sample Interview Questions

When and where did you first meet?
Did you make plans to meet again?
Where is your spouse's hometown?
What are your spouse's parents' names?
Have you met your spouse's parents?
Have you visited your spouse's home country?
When did you decide to get married?
Did you live together before marriage?
When and where did you get married?
How did you get to the ceremony?
How many people attended the ceremony?
May I see your wedding rings?
Did you have a reception after your wedding?
Where did you go for your honeymoon?
Where do you keep the garbage/recycle bins?
What size bed do you have?
How many windows are there in your bedroom?
If you are standing at your stove, where is the refrigerator?

What day is the garbage collected?
Where do you shop for groceries?
What hours does your spouse work?
Have you gone on any trips together?
How much is your monthly rent or mortgage?
What kind of car do you have?
What did you do for Christmas, or other holiday?
Who does the cooking at your house?
What time do you usually eat dinner?
When is your spouse's birthday?
Describe your living room. What color is the ceiling, the carpet, the couch etc.?
Who was your last guest?
What is the last movie you saw together?
How many televisions are in your residence?
Is your residence carpeted?

Signs of a "Sham Marriage"

Immigration Officers are trained to look for the following signs that may indicate a "sham marriage," or a marriage that was entered into for the sake of a Green Card and not out of love.

The foreign spouse was a friend of the U.S. citizen's family before your marriage.
The U.S. Citizen has filed many petitions on behalf of foreign spouses.
You have a significant age gap.
Your marriage is a secret, of which few of your friends or families are aware.
You demonstrate extreme disparity in cultural background.
You and your spouse are unable to communicate.
You do not live together.
You have strongly contrasting religious beliefs.

Your marriage was arranged by a third party, or "matching agency."
You divorced immediately after obtaining a Notice of Action.
You answer the same questions differently.
You lack requested documentation.
You demonstrate a basic lack of trust.

If your marriage is bona fide but demonstrates some of the qualities listed above, it is wise to bring ample evidence with you to the interview that may help overcome any potential suspicions or problems.
For example, if you live separately because of your occupation, (which is a big red flag) bring evidence of your job, and your communication with your spouse such as phone records, emails, letters, visits, trips, etc.

Phase Three – Approval

If the interview goes well, and the Officer is convinced of the good faith of your marriage, permanent residency will be granted as of that day. The Officer will take your EAD card, because it is no longer necessary now that you have permanent resident status. Usually, your Passport will be stamped with the equivalent of a Green Card, and you will be handed a form stating "Pursuant to Section 216 of the Immigration and Nationality Act, you have been granted conditional residence in the United States, as of the date you admitted or adjusted to such status by an Officer of the Citizenship and Immigration Services."

If your Green Card is conditional (if you were married for less than two years before you submitted your original application), then it will expire two years after the day it was granted. You will have a 90-day window to submit evidence that your marriage is genuine and ongoing before the expiration date.

★ **Tip:** During the next two years, it is recommended that you gradually collect evidence of your marriage. The USCIS is looking for the same type of evidence as they were for your initial application and the Interview, but updated.

You should receive your Green Card (permanent resident card) in the mail within two weeks.

Potential Problems

If you bring insufficient documentation

If the Officer determines that documents are missing, they will give you a list of documents they need to examine. Your application will not be approved or denied that day. Usually, a follow-up interview is not scheduled; instead, you will be asked to mail the missing items. Mail the items as soon as possible. If you are late, your entire application may be discarded. After verifying the documents, a written decision will be mailed to you.

If your application arouses suspicion

If the Officer suspects that your marriage is not bona fide, from lack of documentation, a lack of trust between you and your spouse, or inconsistent responses, you may have to endure a **"Stokes Interview."** This consists of you and spouse being interviewed (interrogated) separately, after which the Officer will compare your answers. Usually the Stokes Interview will be scheduled for a later date, but in some cases it might be conducted immediately.

If it is scheduled for a later date, spend ample time reviewing details of your and your spouse's living space and biographic information. Pay extra attention to every detail of your life, such as times, dates, and days of the week that you do things. Talk with your spouse to confirm that you agree about when your first date was, or when you first talked of marriage, etc. In addition, consider hiring an immigration attorney.

The questions asked during the Stokes Interview might be similar to those listed above, but with the added pressure of matching your spouse's answer. Never try to read your spouse's mind, and attempt to answer what you think he or she will answer. Think carefully about each question and answer, only with objective truths. It is far better to admit you do not know or cannot remember something, than to guess or say the wrong thing.

The Officer may accuse the U.S. spouse of criminal activity by filing a petition for a sham marriage. The Officer might even threaten an immigration and customs enforcement investigation. If your marriage is honest, do not panic, an investigation may even help prove your case.

If the examiner denies the Green Card, you will have the chance to appeal the decision before an immigration judge. Do not attempt to appeal without an experienced immigration attorney.

Step IV:
Removing Conditions

Form I-751: Petition to Remove Conditions on Residence

f your Green Card is conditional (if you were married for less than two years before you submitted your original application), then it will expire two years after the day it was granted. The purpose of this form is to remove the two-year conditional status of your Green Card.

★ **Tip:** Begin gathering and collecting evidence of your marriage as soon as you can. This will make the removal of conditions much easier. The USCIS is looking for the same type of evidence as they were for your initial application and the Interview, but updated.

The 90-Day Window

You have a 90-day window prior to the expiration date to submit this form along with evidence that your marriage is genuine.

The USCIS usually **will not** send you any warning or reminder. If you fail to file Form I-751, your Green Card will expire automatically. Submitting as early as possible within the 90-day window is recommended. The USCIS is looking for the same type of marital evidence as they were for the I-130 and the Interview, but updated.

If you miss the I-751 deadline

If you are less than a couple weeks late, mail the application with an explanation. The USCIS may forgive modestly late filings for a "good cause" such as medical problems, family crises, natural disasters, etc. If you are late by more than a couple of weeks, hire a lawyer immediately.

Form I-912 Fee Waiver

The USCIS now permits the filing of Fee Waiver Form I-912, along with Form I-751. To qualify, you must prove that you income is at or below 150% of the poverty line (for 2013 the poverty line is $15,510 so you must have income at or below $23,265), or that you have suffered recent financial hardship. The USCIS requirements and instructions can be found on the official form.

The USCIS updates their forms on occasion. Please visit the USCIS website to ensure that the form you are working on is the most recent. You can easily verify this by looking at the little entry (e.g. Rev. 10/08/10) on the bottom right hand side of any page of any form, and the top right of the first page of instructions (e.g. Expires 10/31/2011).

Download and read the instructions that USCIS provides. Always read the official instructions carefully, especially if your situation is complex. The instructions, like the forms themselves, are revised periodically. If you find a discrepancy between advice offered here and on the official USCIS instructions, follow the latter.

Example Entries

Part 1. Information About You (the foreign spouse)

Family Name (Last Name) **Example:** ADAMS

Given Name (First Name) **Example:** Johanna

Full Middle Name: **Example:** Gottlieb
Address: (Street Number and Name)   Apt. #
Example: 789 Oak Street   33A

City	State/Province	Country	Zip/Postal Code
Example: New York	NY	USA	11220

Mailing Address, if different than above (Street Number and Name):
Enter address if different than above or enter "SAME" in the first box and leave the next six boxes blank.

Date of Birth *(mm/dd/yyyy)* Example: 12/16/1980

Country of Birth Example: Germany

Country of Citizenship Example: Germany

Alien Registration Number Example: 876-543-210

Social Security # Example: 147-25-8369

Conditional Residence Expires on *(mm/dd/yyyy)* Example: 01/24/2013

Daytime Phone # *(Area/Country Code)* Example: (212) 555-2591

Part 2. Basis for Petition *(Check one)*

Under normal marriage based circumstances, check box **a**.

If you have experienced any of the unfortunate situations described in choices **c, d, e, or g**, check the appropriate box and include supporting evidence.

Part 3. Additional Information About You *(Check one)*

1. Other Names Used *(Including maiden name):* (If you have ever been legally known by another name, enter it here) Example: Gottlieb (maiden)

2. Date of Marriage *(mm/dd/yyyy)* Example: 02/14/2009

3. Place of Marriage. Example: Reno, NV, USA

4. If your spouse is deceased, give the date of death *(mm/dd/yyyy)*
   Enter n/a if spouse is living.

   Questions 5-10. If you must check "Yes" to any of the remaining questions, provide a detailed explanation on a separate sheet of paper. Attach the sheet to the back of the form. As with all continuation sheets, include the name/number of the form and the question to which your response refers, your full name, Alien Number (if any), signature and date.

Part 4. Information About the Spouse or Parent Through Whom You Gained Your Conditional Residence

Family Name (Last Name) Example: ADAMS

First Name Example: John

Middle Name Example: Robert

Address Example: 789 Oak Street, Apt. 33A, New York, NY 11220

Date of Birth *(mm/dd/yyyy)* Example: 06/21/1978

Social Security # Example: 012-34-5678

A-Number (Alien Registration Number) *(if any).* Example: "None"

Part 5. Information About Your Children - List All Your Children
(Attach additional sheets if necessary)

Enter your children's biographic information or, if you do not have children, enter "None" in the first name slot and leave the remainder blank.

Part 6. Accommodations for Individuals With Disabilities and Impairments
(Read *the* information in the instructions before completing this section).

If you have any physical handicaps, check the appropriate box and provide details below or on a continuation sheet.

Part 7. Signature

Sign, print your name, date and enter your telephone number then have your spouse do the same.

Part 8. Signature of Person Preparing Form, if other than above

Leave blank, unless someone (such as a lawyer) helped you complete this form.

Attachments for I-751

Identification

Permanent Residence Card (Green **Card**) (front and back)

Passport (recommended)

Evidence of Relationship

Marriage Certificate

Any certificates of divorce or death showing that previous marriages (if any) have been legally terminated

Proof of "cohabitation" such as copies of leases or a mortgage, rent receipts, canceled rent checks from a joint bank account, shared utility bills and anything else to show that you live together. If you live with your parents, as an au pair or in a situation where you do not pay rent, mortgage or utility bills, create a document stating such and have it signed and dated by the appropriate person

Joint bank statements and/or canceled checks from a joint account

Joint investment account statements (CD's, mutual funds, etc.)

Jointly filed Income Tax Returns for the years that you have been married

Shared credit card accounts

Photographs showing you and your spouse together. Photos of you and your spouse with your family, especially during holidays, at your wedding, honeymoon or vacations are particularly convincing.

Joint insurance policies such as health, car, dental, house, life, etc.

Written Affidavits by non-family members confirming your marriage.

Evidence of vacations or trips taken together, such as boarding passes

Anything else that helps prove your marriage is genuine. Emphasize elements that where not submitted in your initial application.

I-751 COVER LETTER TEMPLATE

··

USCIS [City] Service Center
[Full USCIS Address]

[Date]
Re: Petition to Remove Conditions on Residence
[Alien Number]
[Foreign Spouse's Full Name]
[Date of Birth]

Dear USCIS Examiner,

In this packet, you will find my Petition to Remove Conditions on Residence with the following documentation:

- Form I-751
- Check for I-751 Filing Fee
- Copy of Green Card
- Copy of Passport
- Evidence of a bona fide marriage with my U.S. citizen spouse, [Name], organized into the following categories:
  - **I. Proof of joint residence**
  - **II. Family photographs**
  - **III. Comingling of financial liability and assets**
    - a) Jointly filed Federal Tax Returns for [Year]
    - b) [name of bank] joint checking and savings account
    - c) Joint utility Bills
    - d) Lease/mortgage for our shared residence
    - e) Joint Cellular Phone Bills

  - **IV. Affidavits** by two individuals with personal knowledge or our marriage and relationship:
    - a) Sworn affidavit by [Name]
    - b) Sworn affidavit by [Name]

  - **V. Joint insurance benefits**
    - a) Joint [Company Name] health insurance
    - b) Shared [Company Name] Insurance motor vehicle insurance

  - **VI. Miscellaneous**
    - a) Copy of airline tickets for our vacation to [Location] (mm/dd/yyyy – mm/dd/yyyy)
    - b) Copy of [Company/Organization Name] Member cards showing joint membership

Thank you for your consideration.
Sincerely,

[First Name] [Last Name] _____Date_____

[First Name] [Last Name] _____Date_____

One to two weeks after mailing your application, you will receive Notices of Action (NOA) (I-797C) from USCIS. Soon after receiving the NOA, the USCIS will send a detailed ASC (Application Support Center) Appointment Notice about obtaining your Biometrics. This will include a date and location, along with a list of documents to bring with you to the appointment.

The Day of the Biometrics Appointment

> Bring the Appointment Notice NOA (not a copy)

> Bring your current Green Card

> Bring a government issued I.D., such as your Passport and/or your Driver's License

> Bring your Social Security Card (or, at least memorize the number, since you will need it to complete paperwork while at the office)

> Dress appropriately to have your picture taken

> Dress appropriately for the weather, since you may have to wait outside, regardless of the conditions.

> Do not bring cell phones, cameras, or any other electronics into the office. The USCIS is particularly cranky about these devices –leave your phone in the car.

During the Biometrics appointment, an examiner will request to see your hands – palms facing up. They are verifying that your fingers are free of significant cuts or abrasions, and are sufficiently moist. Both of these qualities help ensure accurate fingerprints. If the examiner deems either issue a problem, you will be asked to return on a later date.

Status While Awaiting Your Permanent Resident Card

The receipt notice you receive from the USCIS for your I-751 extends your residency for one year. It is your proof of legal status. You should carry it along with your expired Green Card.

If you end up waiting for your permanent Green Card for more than one year, it will not affect your legal status. However, if you plan to travel outside the U.S., you should get your Passport certified with an I-555 stamp. This will serve as evidence of your legal status. You can do this by scheduling an appointment through INFOPASS, an online USCIS support service. http://infopass.uscis.gov

During the waiting period, you may be called in for an interview. If so, it might indicate the USCIS has doubts about your marriage. In the unlikely event that this happens, consider hiring an immigration attorney.

Receiving your Permanent Resident Card

A few months later, you should receive your Permanent Resident Card in the mail. Now you can rest, the process is over. The only concern you will have is renewing your Green Card every ten years. This is a very simple process, like renewing your driver's license. Congratulations on attaining permanent residency!

Part Two: CHECKLISTS

Part Two: CHECKLISTS

Contents

Use these checklists to organize your application. They will help demystify the requirements and give you the confidence that you have prepared all the necessary ingredients.

Checklist for Initial Filing

Submit *copies* of all official documents. Submit *originals* only when specifically requested by the USCIS

__**Form I-130 completed by U.S. citizen spouse**
__Birth Certificate of foreign spouse (translated)
__Birth Certificate of U.S. citizen spouse (front & back)
__Passport of U.S. citizen spouse (all pages)
__Passport of foreign spouse (all pages)
__Marriage Certificate
__Death/Divorce document of previous marriage (if any)
__1 passport style Color Photo of foreign spouse (labeled)
__1 passport style Color Photo of U.S. citizen spouse (labeled)
__G-325A of foreign spouse (completed and signed)
__G-325A of U.S. citizen spouse

__Proof of joint ownership of property
__Proof of joint residence
__Evidence of joint insurance
__Evidence of shared finances
__Birth certificates of your children (if any)
__Sworn affidavits confirming your marriage (2 - 3)
__Photographs of you and your spouse together
__Other evidence of marriage
__Signature and Date
__Filling Fee of $420
__G-1145: E-Notification of Acceptance (recommended)

__**Form I-485 completed by the foreign spouse**
__Birth Certificate of foreign spouse
__Passport of foreign spouse
__Visa of foreign spouse
__I-94 of foreign spouse (front & back)
__Marriage Certificate
__Death/Divorce document of previous marriage (if any)

__2 passport style Color Photos of foreign spouse (labeled)
__G-325A of foreign spouse
__Criminal history (if any)
__(Fiancé(e) petition approval notice if arrived on K-1 visa)
__Filling Fee of $1070 ($985+$84 for biometrics)
__Signature and Date

__**Form I-864 completed by the U.S. citizen spouse**
__Birth Certificate of U.S. citizen spouse (front & back)
__Passport of U.S. citizen (All pages recommended)
__Tax forms for the three most recent years of U.S. citizen
__Pay stubs for most recent 6 months
__Employer Letter
__(Proof of military status if sponsoring at 100% of the poverty line)
__(Documentation on assets) (if choosing this option)
__Signature and Date

If using income of someone in your household
__ Form I-864A for each person
__Proof of residency in your household
__Tax returns of most recent of the person helping you
__If your spouse is helping, proof that employment will continue from the same source
If using assets of someone in your household
__ Form I-864A for each person (except your spouse)
__Documentation on the assets
If using a joint sponsor or substitute sponsor
__ Form I-864 and same materials as those for the U.S. citizen

__**Form I-693 completed by the foreign spouse**
__Attend medical exam by approved doctor
__Bring Gov. photo ID and Vaccination history to exam

__Sign form in doctor's presence
__Receive completed form from doctor in sealed envelope

Optional forms
__**Form I-765 completed by the foreign spouse**
__2 passport style Color Photos of foreign spouse (labeled)
__Copy of last EAD (front & back) (if any)
__Government photo ID (Passport)
__(Copy of USCIS receipt, if filing separately from main packet)
__Signature and Date

__**Form I-131 completed by the foreign spouse**
__Government photo I.D. (Passport)
__2 passport style color photos of foreign spouse (labeled)
__Advanced parole letter
__(Copy of USCIS receipt, if filing separately from main packet)
__Signature and Date

Assembly

__Single sided printing
__Cover Letter (recommended)
__Well organized
__At least 2 copies of entire package for your records
__Clipped together, not bound or stapled
__"Original Submission" and list of forms written on an envelope
__Delivery Confirmation

Biometrics Checklist

Bring the **originals** of all official documents.

Documents

__Biometrics appointment notice (original)

__Government issued photo ID (passport)

__Marriage Certificate (original)

__Notices of Action for I-130 and I-485 (recommended)

__Social Security Card (you will need your SS# to complete paperwork at the office)

__Alien Registration Number (you will need it to complete paperwork at the office)

Preparation

__Appropriate dress for having your photo taken

__Appropriate dress for the weather conditions in case you or your spouse must wait outside

__Leave all electronics (especially cellular phones) at home or in your car (or at least turned off).

__Try to keep your fingers free of abrasions in the days preceding your appointment

Interview Checklist

Bring the **originals** of all official documents. If you are bringing an official document that was not submitted with your initial application, such as a birth certificate for a recently born child, bring the original document and a copy.

Identification

Foreign Spouse

__Birth Certificate of foreign spouse (with translation)

__Passport of foreign spouse

__Copy of latest EAD (front & back) (if n/a, include Gov. photo ID)

U.S. Spouse

__Birth Certificate of U.S. citizen spouse

__Passport of U.S. citizen spouse (recommended)

Evidence of a "bona fide" marriage"

__Marriage Certificate

__Birth certificates of your children (if any)

__Proof of joint ownership of property

__Proof of joint residence

__Evidence of joint insurance policies such as health, car, dental, house, life etc.

__Evidence of shared finances (bank statements, canceled checks etc.)

__Evidence of shared investments (CD's, mutual funds etc.)

__Evidence of shared credit card accounts (copies of your statements with both names or of both of cards)

__Federal income tax returns for the years you have been married

__Death/Divorce document of previous marriage (if any)

__Photographs of you and your spouse together with and without family members

__Sworn affidavits confirming your marriage (Optional)

__Evidence of vacations/trips taken together (boarding passes, photos etc.)

__Any other documents that support the bona fides of your marriage

Tips

Dress Appropriately

Leave all electronics at home or in your car (or at least turned off)

Be positive and patient

Organize all your documents for easy access

Bring a translator if it will make the foreign spouse more comfortable conversing in English

Consider hiring an attorney to accompany you if your situation is complex.

Know primary biographic information of your spouse such as that entered on form G-325A.

Plan to arrive 30-60 minutes early

Checklist for I-751

Petition to Remove Conditions On Residence

Submit *copies* of all official documents. Submit *originals* only when specifically requested by the USCIS

Identification
__Permanent Resident Card

__Passport (foreign spouse)

Evidence of Relationship
__Proof of joint ownership of property

__Proof of joint residence

__Evidence of joint insurance

__Evidence of shared finances

__Birth certificates of your children (if any)

__Sworn affidavits confirming your marriage (2 - 3)

__Photographs of you and your spouse together

__Any other documents that support the bona fides of your marriage

__Signature and Date

__(Form I-912 Fee Waiver (Optional))

__Filling Fee of $590 ($505 + $85 for biometrics) (or adjust based on Fee Waiver if applicable)

__G-1145: E-Notification of Application/Petition Acceptance (recommended)

Assembly
__Single sided printing

__Well organized

__Cover Letter (recommended)

__At least 2 copies of entire package for your records

__Clipped together, not bond or stapled

__"Re: Petition to remove conditions on residence" written on the envelope

__Delivery Confirmation

Part Three:
EXAMPLE ENTRIES

Part Three: EXAMPLE ENTRIES

Contents

Use these completed forms as cheat sheets to see exactly what USCIS is asking for. Simply replace the examples answers with your own information.

Department of Homeland Security
U.S. Citizenship and Immigration Services

OMB #1615-0012; Expires 01/31/2011

I-130, Petition for Alien Relative

DO NOT WRITE IN THIS BLOCK - FOR USCIS OFFICE ONLY

A#	Action Stamp	Fee Stamp

Section of Law/Visa Category
- [ ] 201(b) Spouse - IR-1/CR-1
- [ ] 201(b) Child - IR-2/CR-2
- [ ] 201(b) Parent - IR-5
- [ ] 203(a)(1) Unm. S or D - F1-1
- [ ] 203(a)(2)(A)Spouse - F2-1
- [ ] 203(a)(2)(A) Child - F2-2
- [ ] 203(a)(2)(B) Unm. S or D - F2-4
- [ ] 203(a)(3) Married S or D - F3-1
- [ ] 203(a)(4) Brother/Sister - F4-1

Petition was filed on: _____ (priority date)
- [ ] Personal Interview
- [ ] Pet.
- [ ] Ben. " A" File Reviewed
- [ ] Field Investigation
- [ ] 203(a)(2)(A) Resolved
- [ ] Previously Forwarded
- [ ] I-485 Filed Simultaneously
- [ ] 204(g) Resolved
- [ ] 203(g) Resolved

Remarks:

A. Relationship   You are the petitioner.   Your relative is the beneficiary.

1. I am filing this petition for my:
- [x] Husband/Wife
- [ ] Parent
- [ ] Brother/Sister
- [ ] Child

2. Are you related by adoption?
- [ ] Yes
- [x] No

3. Did you gain permanent residence through adoption?
- [ ] Yes
- [x] No

B. Information about you

1. Name (Family name in CAPS) (First) (Middle)
ADAMS   John   Robert

2. Address (Number and Street) (Apt. No.)
789 Oak Street   33A

(Town or City) (State/Country) (Zip/Postal Code)
New York   NY   11220

3. Place of Birth (Town or City) (State/Country)
Brookline   MA

4. Date of Birth
06/21/1978

5. Gender
- [x] Male
- [ ] Female

6. Marital Status
- [x] Married
- [ ] Widowed
- [ ] Single
- [ ] Divorced

7. Other Names Used (including maiden name)
None

8. Date and Place of Present Marriage (if married)
02/14/2009   Reno NV USA

9. U.S. Social Security Number (If any)
012-34-5678

10. Alien Registration Number
None

11. Name(s) of Prior Husband(s)/Wive(s)
Janet BENNET

12. Date(s) Marriage(s) Ended
12/21/2004

13. If you are a U.S. citizen, complete the following:

My citizenship was acquired through (check one):
- [x] Birth in the U.S.
- [ ] Naturalization. Give certificate number and date and place of issuance.

_____

- [ ] Parents. Have you obtained a certificate of citizenship in your own name?
  - [ ] Yes. Give certificate number, date and place of issuance.
  - [ ] No

14. If you are a lawful permanent resident alien, complete the following:

Date and place of admission for or adjustment to lawful permanent residence and class of admission.

14b. Did you gain permanent resident status through marriage to a U.S. citizen or lawful permanent resident?
- [ ] Yes
- [x] No

C. Information about your relative

1. Name (Family name in CAPS) (First) (Middle)
ADAMS   Johanna   Gottlieb

2.Address (Number and Street) (Apt. No.)
789 Oak Street   33A

(Town or City) (State/Country) (Zip/Postal Code)
New York   NY   11220

3. Place of Birth (Town or City) (State/Country)
Hamburg   Germany

4. Date of Birth
12/16/1980

5. Gender
- [ ] Male
- [x] Female

6. Marital Status
- [x] Married
- [ ] Widowed
- [ ] Single
- [ ] Divorced

7. Other Names Used (including maiden name)
GOTTLIEB (maiden)

8. Date and Place of Present Marriage (if married)
02/14/2009   Reno, NV USA

9. U.S. Social Security Number (If any)
147-25-8369

10. Alien Registration Number
876-543-210

11. Name(s) of Prior Husband(s)/Wive(s)
Ditters von DITTERSDORF

12. Date(s) Marriage(s) Ended
03/16/2007

13. Has your relative ever been in the U.S.?
- [x] Yes
- [ ] No

14. If your relative is currently in the U.S., complete the following:

He or she arrived as a:
(visitor, student, stowaway, without inspection, etc.)   K-3

Arrival/Departure Record (I-94)
2 1 2 ▬ 6 8 0 5 6 8 0 5

Date arrived
11/20/2009

Date authorized stay expired, or will expire, as shown on Form I-94 or I-95
11/20/2011

15. Name and address of present employer (if any)
None

Date this employment began

16. Has your relative ever been under immigration proceedings?
- [x] No
- [ ] Yes Where _____ When _____
- [ ] Removal
- [ ] Exclusion/Deportation
- [ ] Rescission
- [ ] Judicial Proceedings

INITIAL RECEIPT	RESUBMITTED	RELOCATED: Rec'd _____	Sent _____	COMPLETED: Appv'd _____	Denied _____	Ret'd _____

C. Information about your alien relative (continued)

17. List husband/wife and all children of your relative.

(Name)	(Relationship)	(Date of Birth)	(Country of Birth)
John Robert ADAMS	Husband	06/21/1978	USA

---

18. Address in the United States where your relative intends to live.

(Street Address)	(Town or City)	(State)
789 Oak Street	New York	NY

19. Your relative's address abroad. (Include street, city, province and country)   Phone Number (if any)

Kieler Strasse 1211 D-22543 Hamburg, Germany   31207125601

20. If your relative's native alphabet is other than Roman letters, write his or her name and foreign address in the native alphabet.

(Name)   Address (Include street, city, province and country):

Same   Kieler Straße 1211 D-22543 Hamburg Germany

21. If filing for your husband/wife, give last address at which you lived together. (Include street, city, province, if any, and country):

	From:	**To:**
789 Oak Street New York, NY 11220	11/20/2009	Present

22. Complete the information below if your relative is in the United States and will apply for adjustment of status.

Your relative is in the United States and will apply for adjustment of status to that of a lawful permanent resident at the USCIS office in:

If your relative is not eligible for adjustment of status, he or she will apply for a visa abroad at the American consular post in:

New York	NY	n/a	
(City)	(State)	(City)	(Country

NOTE: Designation of a U.S. embassy or consulate outside the country of your relative's last residence does not guarantee acceptance for processing by that post. Acceptance is at the discretion of the designated embassy or consulate.

D. Other information

1. If separate petitions are also being submitted for other relatives, give names of each and relationship.

None

2. Have you ever before filed a petition for this or any other alien?   ☐ Yes   ☒ No

If "Yes," give name, place and date of filing and result.

WARNING: USCIS investigates claimed relationships and verifies the validity of documents. USCIS seeks criminal prosecutions when family relationships are falsified to obtain visas.

PENALTIES: By law, you may be imprisoned for not more than five years or fined $250,000, or both, for entering into a marriage contract for the purpose of evading any provision of the immigration laws. In addition, you may be fined up to $10,000 and imprisoned for up to five years, or both, for knowingly and willfully falsifying or concealing a material fact or using any false document in submitting this petition.

YOUR CERTIFICATION: I certify, under penalty of perjury under the laws of the United States of America, that the foregoing is true and correct. Furthermore, I authorize the release of any information from my records that U.S. Citizenship and Immigration Services needs to determine eligiblity for the benefit that I am seeking.

E. Signature of petitioner.

Date   Phone Number (212) 555-2591

F. Signature of person preparing this form, if other than the petitioner.

I declare that I prepared this document at the request of the person above and that it is based on all information of which I have any knowledge.

Print Name _____   Signature _____   Date _____

Address _____   **G-28 ID or VOLAG Number, if any.** _____

(Family Name)	(First Name)	(Middle Name)	☐ Male ☒ Female	Date of Birth (mm/dd/yyyy)	Citizenship/Nationality	File Number
ADAMS	Johanna	Gottlieb		12/16/1980	Germany	A 876-543-210

All Other Names Used (include names by previous marriages)	City and Country of Birth	U.S. Social Security # *(if any)*
GOTTLIEB -maiden, DITTERSDORF -prior marriage	Hamburg, Germany	147-25-8369

	Family Name	First Name	Date of Birth (mm/dd/yyyy)	City, and Country of Birth (if known)	City and Country of Residence
Father	GOTTLIEB	Karl	08/04/1951	Hamburg, Germany	Hamburg, Germany
Mother (Maiden Name)	SCHUMANN	Clara	01/12/1954	Hamburg, Germany	Hamburg, Germany

Current Husband or Wife (If none, so state) Family Name (For wife, give maiden name)	First Name	Date of Birth (mm/dd/yyyy)	City and Country of Birth	Date of Marriage	Place of Marriage
ADAMS	John	06/21/1978	Brookline, USA	02/14/2009	Reno, NV

Former Husbands or Wives (If none, so state) Family Name (For wife, give maiden name)	First Name	Date of Birth (mm/dd/yyyy)	Date and Place of Marriage	Date and Place of Termination of Marriage
DITTERSDORF	Ditters	11/02/1979	04/11/2000 Germany	03/16/2007 Germany

Applicant's residence last five years. List present address first.

Street and Number	City	Province or State	Country	From Month	From Year	To Month	To Year
789 Oak Street	New York	NY	USA	11	2009	Present Time	

Applicant's last address outside the United States of more than 1 year.

Street and Number	City	Province or State	Country	From Month	From Year	To Month	To Year
Kieler Straße 1211 D-22543	Hamburg		Germany	05	1984	11	2009

Applicant's employment last five years. (If none, so state.) List present employment first.

Full Name and Address of Employer	Occupation (Specify)	From Month	From Year	To Month	To Year
None				Present Time	

Last occupation abroad if not shown above. (Include all information requested above.)

This form is submitted in connection with an application for:	Signature of Applicant	Date
☐ Naturalization ☐ Other (Specify): ☒ Status as Permanent Resident		

If your native alphabet is in other than Roman letters, write your name in your native alphabet below:

Penalties: Severe penalties are provided by law for knowingly and willfully falsifying or concealing a material fact.

Applicant: Print your name and Alien Registration Number in the box outlined by heavy border below.

Complete This Box (Family Name)	(Given Name)	(Middle Name)	(Alien Registration Number)
ADAMS	Johanna	Gottlieb	A 876-543-210

Form G-325A (Rev. 06/12/09)Y

Instructions

Complete this biographical information form and include it with the application or petition you are submitting to U.S. Citizenship and Immigration Services (USCIS).

USCIS will use the information you provide on this form to process your application or petition.

If you have any questions on how to complete the form, call our National Customer Service Center at **1-800-375-5283**.

We ask for the information on this form, and associated evidence, to determine if you have established eligibility for the immigration benefit for which you are filing. Our legal right to ask for this information can be found in the Immigration and Nationality Act, as amended. We may provide this information to other government agencies. Failure to provide this information, and any requested evidence, may delay a final decision or result in denial of your immigration benefit.

An agency may not conduct or sponsor an information collection and a person is not required to respond to a collection of information unless it displays a currently valid OMB control number. The public reporting burden for this collection of information is estimated at 15 minutes per response, including the time for reviewing instructions and completing and submitting the form. Send comments regarding this burden estimate or any other aspect of this collection of information, including suggestions for reducing this burden, to: U.S. Citizenship and Immigration Services, Regulatory Products Division, 111 Massachusetts Avenue, N.W., 3rd Floor, Suite 3008, Washington, DC 20529-2210. OMB No. 1615-0008. **Do not mail your application to this address.**

(Family Name) ADAMS	(First Name) John	(Middle Name) Robert	☒ Male ☐ Female	Date of Birth (mm/dd/yyyy) 06/21/1978	Citizenship/Nationality USA	File Number **A** None

All Other Names Used (include names by previous marriages) None	City and Country of Birth Brookline USA	U.S. Social Security # *(if any)* 012-34-5678

	Family Name	First Name	Date of Birth (mm/dd/yyyy)	City, and Country of Birth (if known)	City and Country of Residence
Father	ADAMS	Jacob	08/11/1952	New York, USA	New York, USA
Mother (Maiden Name)	JOHNSON	Sarah	01/04/1955	Huntington, USA	New York, USA

Current Husband or Wife (If none, so state) Family Name (For wife, give maiden name) GOTTLIEB	First Name Johanna	Date of Birth (mm/dd/yyyy) 12/16/1980	City and Country of Birth Hamburg, German	Date of Marriage 02/14/2009	Place of Marriage Reno, NV

Former Husbands or Wives (If none, so state) Family Name (For wife, give maiden name) BENNETT	First Name Janet	Date of Birth (mm/dd/yyyy) 03/13/1978	Date and Place of Marriage 05/04/2000 NY, USA	Date and Place of Termination of Marriage 12/21/2004 NY, USA

Applicant's residence last five years. List present address first.

Street and Number	City	Province or State	Country	From Month	From Year	To Month	To Year
789 Oak Street	New York	NY	USA	09	2005	**Present Time**	

Applicant's last address outside the United States of more than 1 year.

Street and Number	City	Province or State	Country	From Month	From Year	To Month	To Year
None							

Applicant's employment last five years. (If none, so state.) List present employment first.

Full Name and Address of Employer	Occupation (Specify)	From Month	From Year	To Month	To Year
Top Quality Heating and Cooling, Greenwich, CT	Plumber	05	1998	**Present Time**	

Last occupation abroad if not shown above. (Include all information requested above.)

This form is submitted in connection with an application for: ☐ Naturalization ☐ Other (Specify): ☒ Status as Permanent Resident	Signature of Applicant	Date

If your native alphabet is in other than Roman letters, write your name in your native alphabet below:

Penalties: Severe penalties are provided by law for knowingly and willfully falsifying or concealing a material fact.

Applicant: Print your name and Alien Registration Number in the box outlined by heavy border below.

Complete This Box (Family Name) ADAMS	(Given Name) John	(Middle Name) Robert	(Alien Registration Number) **A** None

Form G-325A (Rev. 06/12/09)Y

Instructions

███

Complete this biographical information form and include it with the application or petition you are submitting to U.S. Citizenship and Immigration Services (USCIS).

USCIS will use the information you provide on this form to process your application or petition.

If you have any questions on how to complete the form, call our National Customer Service Center at **1-800-375-5283**.

███

We ask for the information on this form, and associated evidence, to determine if you have established eligibility for the immigration benefit for which you are filing. Our legal right to ask for this information can be found in the Immigration and Nationality Act, as amended. We may provide this information to other government agencies. Failure to provide this information, and any requested evidence, may delay a final decision or result in denial of your immigration benefit.

███

An agency may not conduct or sponsor an information collection and a person is not required to respond to a collection of information unless it displays a currently valid OMB control number. The public reporting burden for this collection of information is estimated at 15 minutes per response, including the time for reviewing instructions and completing and submitting the form. Send comments regarding this burden estimate or any other aspect of this collection of information, including suggestions for reducing this burden, to: U.S. Citizenship and Immigration Services, Regulatory Products Division, 111 Massachusetts Avenue, N.W., 3rd Floor, Suite 3008, Washington, DC 20529-2210. OMB No. 1615-0008. **Do not mail your application to this address.**

START HERE - Type or Print (Use black ink)

Part 1. Information About You

For USCIS Use Only	
Returned	Receipt

Family Name *(Last Name)*
ADAMS

Given Name *(First Name)*
Johanna

Middle Name
Gottlieb

Address - Street Number and Name
789 Oak Street

Apt. #
33A

C/O *(in care of)*

City
New York

State
NY

Zip Code
11220

Date of Birth *(mm/dd/yyyy)*
12/16/1980

Country of Birth
Germany

Country of Citizenship/Nationality
Germany

U.S. Social Security # *(if any)*
147-25-8369

A # *(if any)*
876-543-210

Date of Last Arrival *(mm/dd/yyyy)*
11/20/2009

I-94 #
212680568 05

Current USCIS Status
K-3

Expires on *(mm/dd/yyyy)*
11/20/2011

Resubmitted

Reloc Sent

Reloc Rec'd

**Applicant
Interviewed**

Part 2. Application Type *(Check one)*

I am applying for an adjustment to permanent resident status because:

a. ☒ An immigrant petition giving me an immediately available immigrant visa number that has been approved. (Attach a copy of the approval notice, or a relative, special immigrant juvenile, or special immigrant military visa petition filed with this application that will give you an immediately available visa number, if approved.)

b. ☐ My spouse or parent applied for adjustment of status or was granted lawful permanent residence in an immigrant visa category that allows derivative status for spouses and children.

c. ☐ I entered as a K-1 fiancé(e) of a U.S. citizen whom I married within 90 days of entry, or I am the K-2 child of such a fiancé(e). (Attach a copy of the fiancé(e) petition approval notice and the marriage certificate.)

d. ☐ I was granted asylum or derivative asylum status as the spouse or child of a person granted asylum and am eligible for adjustment.

e. ☐ I am a native or citizen of Cuba admitted or paroled into the United States after January 1, 1959, and thereafter have been physically present in the United States for at least 1 year.

f. ☐ I am the husband, wife, or minor unmarried child of a Cuban described above in **(e),** and I am residing with that person, and was admitted or paroled into the United States after January 1, 1959, and thereafter have been physically present in the United States for at least 1 year.

g. ☐ I have continuously resided in the United States since before January 1, 1972.

h. ☐ Other basis of eligibility. Explain (for example, I was admitted as a refugee, my status has not been terminated, and I have been physically present in the United States for 1 year after admission). If additional space is needed, see **Page 2** of the instructions. _____

I am already a permanent resident and am applying to have the date I was granted permanent residence adjusted to the date I originally arrived in the United States as a nonimmigrant or parolee, or as of May 2, 1964, whichever date is later, and: *(Check one)*

i. ☐ I am a native or citizen of Cuba and meet the description in **(e)** above.

j. ☐ I am the husband, wife, or minor unmarried child of a Cuban and meet the description in **(f)** above.

Section of Law
☐ Sec. 209(a), INA
☐ Sec. 209(b), INA
☐ Sec. 13, Act of 9/11/57
☐ Sec. 245, INA
☐ Sec. 249, INA
☐ Sec. 1 Act of 11/2/66
☐ Sec. 2 Act of 11/2/66
☐ Other _____

Country Chargeable

Eligibility Under Sec. 245
☐ Approved Visa Petition
☐ Dependent of Principal Alien
☐ Special Immigrant
☐ Other _____

Preference

Action Block

To be Completed by
Attorney or Representative, **if any**
☐ Fill in box if Form G-28 is attached to represent the applicant.

VOLAG #

ATTY State License #

Part 3. Processing Information

A.

City/Town/Village of Birth

Hamburg

Current Occupation

Oboist

Your Mother's First Name

Clara

Your Father's First Name

Karl

Give your name exactly as it appears on your Form I-94, Arrival-Departure Record

Johanna GOTTLIEB

Place of Last Entry Into the United States *(City/State)*

New York, NY

In what status did you last enter? *(Visitor, student, exchange visitor, crewman, temporary worker, without inspection, etc.)*

K-3

Were you inspected by a U.S. Immigration Officer?   Yes ☒   No ☐

Nonimmigrant Visa Number

12345678

Consulate Where Visa Was Issued

Hamburg, Germany

Date Visa Issued *(mm/dd/yyyy)*

11/01/2009

Gender   ☐ Male ☒ Female

Marital Status   ☒ Married ☐ Single ☐ Divorced ☐ Widowed

Have you ever applied for permanent resident status in the U.S.?   ☐ Yes *(If "Yes" give date and place of filing and final disposition.)*   ☒ No

B. List your present spouse and all of your children (include adult sons and daughters). (If you have none, write "None." If additional space is needed, see **Page 2** of the instructions.)

Family Name *(Last Name)*	Given Name *(First Name)*	Middle Initial	Date of Birth *(mm/dd/yyyy)*
ADAMS	John	R	06/21/1978
Country of Birth	Relationship	A # *(if any)*	Applying with you?
USA	Husband		Yes ☐ No ☒
Family Name *(Last Name)*	Given Name *(First Name)*	Middle Initial	Date of Birth *(mm/dd/yyyy)*
Country of Birth	Relationship	A # *(if any)*	Applying with you?
			Yes ☐ No ☐
Family Name *(Last Name)*	Given Name *(First Name)*	Middle Initial	Date of Birth *(mm/dd/yyyy)*
Country of Birth	Relationship	A # *(if any)*	Applying with you?
			Yes ☐ No ☐
Family Name *(Last Name)*	Given Name *(First Name)*	Middle Initial	Date of Birth *(mm/dd/yyyy)*
Country of Birth	Relationship	A # *(if any)*	Applying with you?
			Yes ☐ No ☐
Family Name *(Last Name)*	Given Name *(First Name)*	Middle Initial	Date of Birth *(mm/dd/yyyy)*
Country of Birth	Relationship	A # *(if any)*	Applying with you?
			Yes ☐ No ☐

Form I-485 (Rev. 11/23/10) Y Page 2

Part 3. Processing Information *(Continued)*

C. List your present and past membership in or affiliation with every organization, association, fund, foundation, party, club, society, or similar group in the United States or in other places since your 16th birthday. Include **any military service** in this part. If none, write "None." Include the name of each organization, location, nature, and dates of membership. If additional space is needed, attach a separate sheet of paper. Continuation pages must be submitted according to the guidelines provided on **Page 2** of the instructions under "What Are the General Filing Instructions?"

Name of Organization	Location and Nature	Date of Membership From	Date of Membership To
None			

Answer the following questions. (If your answer is **"Yes"** to any question, explain on a separate piece of paper. Continuation pages must be submitted according to the guidelines provided on **Page 2** of the instructions under "What Are the General Filing Instructions?" Information about documentation that must be include with your application is also provide in this section.) Answering **"Yes"** does not necessarily mean that you are not entitled to adjust status or register for permanent residence.

1. Have you **EVER**, in or outside the United States:

    a. Knowingly committed any crime of moral turpitude or a drug-related offense for which you have not been arrested?   Yes ☐ No ☒

    b. Been arrested, cited, charged, indicted, convicted, fined, or imprisoned for breaking or violating any law or ordinance, excluding traffic violations?   Yes ☐ No ☒

    c. Been the beneficiary of a pardon, amnesty, rehabilitation decree, other act of clemency, or similar action?   Yes ☐ No ☒

    d. Exercised diplomatic immunity to avoid prosecution for a criminal offense in the United States?   Yes ☐ No ☒

2. Have you received public assistance in the United States from any source, including the U.S. Government or any State, county, city, or municipality (other than emergency medical treatment), or are you likely to receive public assistance in the future?   Yes ☐ No ☒

3. Have you **EVER**:

    a. Within the past 10 years been a prostitute or procured anyone for prostitution, or intend to engage in such activities in the future?   Yes ☐ No ☒

    b. Engaged in any unlawful commercialized vice, including, but not limited to, illegal gambling?   Yes ☐ No ☒

    c. Knowingly encouraged, induced, assisted, abetted, or aided any alien to try to enter the United States illegally?   Yes ☐ No ☒

    d. Illicitly trafficked in any controlled substance, or knowingly assisted, abetted, or colluded in the illicit trafficking of any controlled substance?   Yes ☐ No ☒

4. Have you **EVER** engaged in, conspired to engage in, or do you intend to engage in, or have you ever solicited membership or funds for, or have you through any means ever assisted or provided any type of material support to any person or organization that has ever engaged or conspired to engage in sabotage, kidnapping, political assassination, hijacking, or any other form of terrorist activity?   Yes ☐ No ☒

5. Do you intend to engage in the United States in:

   a. Espionage?   Yes ☐   No ☒

   b. Any activity a purpose of which is opposition to, or the control or overthrow of, the Government of the United States, by force, violence, or other unlawful means?   Yes ☐   No ☒

   c. Any activity to violate or evade any law prohibiting the export from the United States of goods, technology, or sensitive information?   Yes ☐   No ☒

6. Have you **EVER** been a member of, or in any way affiliated with, the Communist Party or any other totalitarian party?   Yes ☐   No ☒

7. Did you, during the period from March 23, 1933, to May 8, 1945, in association with either the Nazi Government of Germany or any organization or government associated or allied with the Nazi Government of Germany, ever order, incite, assist, or otherwise participate in the persecution of any person because of race, religion, national origin, or political opinion?   Yes ☐   No ☒

8. Have you **EVER** been deported from the United States, or removed from the United States at government expense, excluded within the past year, or are you now in exclusion, deportation, removal, or rescission proceedings?   Yes ☐   No ☒

9. Are you under a final order of civil penalty for violating section 274C of the Immigration and Nationality Act for use of fraudulent documents or have you, by fraud or willful misrepresentation of a material fact, ever sought to procure, or procured, a visa, other documentation, entry into the United States, or any immigration benefit?   Yes ☐   No ☒

10. Have you **EVER** left the United States to avoid being drafted into the U.S. Armed Forces?   Yes ☐   No ☒

11. Have you **EVER** been a J nonimmigrant exchange visitor who was subject to the 2-year foreign residence requirement and have not yet complied with that requirement or obtained a waiver?   Yes ☐   No ☒

12. Are you now withholding custody of a U.S. citizen child outside the United States from a person granted custody of the child?   Yes ☐   No ☒

13. Do you plan to practice polygamy in the United States?   Yes ☐   No ☒

14. Have you **EVER** ordered, incited, called for, committed, assisted, helped with, or otherwise participated in any of the following:

   a. Acts involving torture or genocide?   Yes ☐   No ☒

   b. Killing any person?   Yes ☐   No ☒

   c. Intentionally and severely injuring any person?   Yes ☐   No ☒

   d. Engaging in any kind of sexual contact or relations with any person who was being forced or threatened?   Yes ☐   No ☒

   e. Limiting or denying any person's ability to exercise religious beliefs?   Yes ☐   No ☒

15. Have you **EVER**:

   a. Served in, been a member of, assisted in, or participated in any military unit, paramilitary unit, police unit, self-defense unit, vigilante unit, rebel group, guerrilla group, militia, or insurgent organization?   Yes ☐   No ☒

   b. Served in any prison, jail, prison camp, detention facility, labor camp, or any other situation that involved detaining persons?   Yes ☐   No ☒

16. Have you **EVER** been a member of, assisted in, or participated in any group, unit, or organization of any kind in which you or other persons used any type of weapon against any person or threatened to do so?   Yes ☐   No ☒

Part 3. Processing Information *(Continued)*

17. Have you **EVER** assisted or participated in selling or providing weapons to any person who to your knowledge used them against another person, or in transporting weapons to any person who to your knowledge used them against another person?   Yes ☐   No ☒

18. Have you **EVER** received any type of military, paramilitary, or weapons training?   Yes ☐   No ☒

Part 4. Accommodations for Individuals With Disabilities and/or Impairments *(See **Page 10** of the instructions before completing this section.)*

Are you requesting an accommodation because of your disability(ies) and/or impairment(s)?   Yes ☐   No ☒

If you answered "Yes," check any applicable box:

☐ **a.** I am deaf or hard of hearing and request the following accommodation(s) (if requesting a sign-language interpreter, indicate which language (e.g., American Sign Language)):

☐ **b.** I am blind or sight-impaired and request the following accommodation(s):

☐ **c.** I have another type of disability and/or impairment (describe the nature of your disability(ies) and/or impairment(s) and accommodation(s) you are requesting):

Part 5. Signature *(Read the information on penalties on **Page 10** of the instructions before completing this section. You must file this application while in the United States.)*

Your Registration With U.S. Citizenship and Immigration Services

"I understand and acknowledge that, under section 262 of the Immigration and Nationality Act (INA), as an alien who has been or will be in the United States for more than 30 days, I am required to register with U.S. Citizenship and Immigration Services (USCIS). I understand and acknowledge that, under section 265 of the INA, I am required to provide USCIS with my current address and written notice of any change of address within **10** days of the change. I understand and acknowledge that USCIS will use the most recent address that I provide to USCIS, on any form containing these acknowledgements, for all purposes, including the service of a Notice to Appear should it be necessary for USCIS to initiate removal proceedings against me. I understand and acknowledge that if I change my address without providing written notice to USCIS, I will be held responsible for any communications sent to me at the most recent address that I provided to USCIS. I further understand and acknowledge that, if removal proceedings are initiated against me and I fail to attend any hearing, including an initial hearing based on service of the Notice to Appear at the most recent address that I provided to USCIS or as otherwise provided by law, I may be ordered removed in my absence, arrested, and removed from the United States."

Selective Service Registration

The following applies to you if you are a male at least 18 years of age, but not yet 26 years of age, who is required to register with the Selective Service System: "I understand that my filing Form I-485 with U.S. Citizenship and Immigration Services (USCIS) authorizes USCIS to provide certain registration information to the Selective Service System in accordance with the Military Selective Service Act. Upon USCIS acceptance of my application, I authorize USCIS to transmit to the Selective Service System my name, current address, Social Security Number, date of birth, and the date I filed the application for the purpose of recording my Selective Service registration as of the filing date. If, however, USCIS does not accept my application, I further understand that, if so required, I am responsible for registering with the Selective Service by other means, provided I have not yet reached 26 years of age."

Part 5. Signature *(Continued)*

Applicant's Statement *(Check one)*

☒ I can read and understand English, and I have read and understand each and every question and instruction on this form, as well as my answer to each question.

☐ Each and every question and instruction on this form, as well as my answer to each question, has been read to me in the _____ language, a language in which I am fluent, by the person named in **Interpreter's Statement and Signature**. I understand each and every question and instruction on this form, as well as my answer to each question.

I certify, under penalty of perjury under the laws of the United States of America, that the information provided with this application is all true and correct. I certify also that I have not withheld any information that would affect the outcome of this application.

I authorize the release of any information from my records that U.S. Citizenship and Immigration Services (USCIS) needs to determine eligibility for the benefit I am seeking.

Signature *(Applicant)*	**Print Your Full Name**	**Date** *(mm/dd/yyyy)*	**Daytime Phone Number** *(include area code)*

NOTE: *If you do not completely fill out this form or fail to submit required documents listed in the instructions, you may not be found eligible for the requested benefit, and this application may be denied.*

Interpreter's Statement and Signature

I certify that I am fluent in English and the below-mentioned language.

Language Used *(language in which applicant is fluent)*

I further certify that I have read each and every question and instruction on this form, as well as the answer to each question, to this applicant in the above-mentioned language, and the applicant has understood each and every instruction and question on the form, as well as the answer to each question.

Signature *(Interpreter)*	**Print Your Full Name**	**Date** *(mm/dd/yyyy)*	**Phone Number** *(include area code)*

Part 6. Signature of Person Preparing Form, If Other Than Above

I declare that I prepared this application at the request of the above applicant, and it is based on all information of which I have knowledge.

Signature	**Print Your Full Name**	**Date** *(mm/dd/yyyy)*	**Phone Number** *(include area code)*

Firm Name and Address	E-Mail Address *(if any)*

Department of Homeland Security
U.S. Citizenship and Immigration Services

I-864, Affidavit of Support
Under Section 213A of the Act

Part 1. Basis for filing Affidavit of Support.

1. I, John Robert ADAMS   ,

am the sponsor submitting this affidavit of support because (Check only one box):

a. ☒ **I am the petitioner. I filed or am filing for the immigration of my relative.**

b. ☐ **I filed an alien worker petition on behalf of the intending immigrant, who is related to me as my** _____

c. ☐ **I have an ownership interest of at least 5 percent in** _____ , **which filed an alien worker petition on behalf of the intending immigrant, who is related to me as my** _____

d. ☐ **I am the only joint sponsor.**

e. ☐ **I am the ☐ first ☐ second of two joint sponsors.** *(Check appropriate box.)*

f. ☐ **The original petitioner is deceased. I am the substitute sponsor. I am the intending immigrant's** _____ .

This I-864 is from:
☐ the Petitioner
☐ a Joint Sponsor #
_____
☐ the Substitute Sponsor
☐ 5% Owner

This I-864:

☐ does not meet the requirements of section 213A.

☐ meets the requirements of section 213A.

_____
Reviewer

_____
Location

_____
Date *(mm/dd/yyyy)*

Part 2. Information on the principal immigrant.

2. Last Name   ADAMS

First Name	Middle Name
Johanna	Gottlieb

3. Mailing Address Street Number and Name *(Include Apartment Number)*

789 Oak Street, Apt. 33A

City	State/Province	Zip/Postal Code	Country
New York	NY	11220	USA

4. Country of Citizenship	**5.** Date of Birth *(mm/dd/yyyy)*
Germany	12/16/1980

6. Alien Registration Number *(if any)*	**7.** U.S. Social Security Number *(if any)*
A- 876-543-210	147-25-8369

Number of Affidavits of Support in file:

☐ 1   ☐ 2

Part 3. Information on the immigrant(s) you are sponsoring.

8. ☒ I am sponsoring the principal immigrant named in Part 2 above.

☒ Yes   ☐ No (Applicable only in cases with two joint sponsors)

9. ☐ I am sponsoring the following family members immigrating at the same time or within six months of the principal immigrant named in **Part 2** above. Do not include any relative listed on a separate visa petition.

Name	Relationship to Sponsored Immigrant	Date of Birth *(mm/dd/yyyy)*	A-Number *(if any)*	U.S.Social Security Number *(if any)*
a.				
b.				
c.				
d.				
e.				

10. Enter the total number of immigrants you are sponsoring on this form from **Part 3**, Items **8** and **9**. | 0 | 1 |

Form I-864 (Rev. 10/08/10)Y

Part 4. Information on the Sponsor.

11. Name	Last Name	
	ADAMS	
	First Name	Middle Name
	John	Robert

12. Mailing Address	Street Number and Name *(Include Apartment Number)*	
	789 Oak Street, Apt. 33A	
	City	State or Province
	New York	NY
	Country	Zip/Postal Code
	USA	11220

13. Place of Residence *(if different from mailing address)*	Street Number and Name *(Include Apartment Number)*	
	SAME	
	City	State or Province
	Country	Zip/Postal Code

14. Telephone Number *(Include Area Code or Country and City Codes)*

(212) 555-2591

15. Country of Domicile

USA

16. Date of Birth *(mm/dd/yyyy)*

06/21/1978

17. Place of Birth *(City)*	State or Province	Country
Brookline	MA	USA

18. U.S. Social Security Number *(Required)*

012-34-5678

19. Citizenship/Residency

[X] I am a U.S. citizen.

[ ] I am a U.S. national (for joint sponsors only).

[ ] I am a lawful permanent resident. My alien registration number is A-_____

If you checked box (b), (c), (d), (e) or (f) in line 1 on Page 1, you must include proof of your citizen, national, or permanent resident status.

20. Military Service (To be completed by petitioner sponsors only.)

I am currently on active duty in the U.S. armed services.　　[ ] Yes　　[X] No

Part 5. Sponsor's household size.

21. Your Household Size - <u>DO NOT COUNT ANYONE TWICE</u>

Persons you are sponsoring in this affidavit:

    a. Enter the number you entered on line 10.   `0` `1`

Persons NOT sponsored in this affidavit:

    b. Yourself.   **1**

    c. If you are currently married, enter "1" for your spouse.   `0`

    d. If you have dependent children, enter the number here.   `0`

    e. If you have any other dependents, enter the number here.   `0`

    f. If you have sponsored any other persons on an I-864 or I-864 EZ who are now lawful permanent residents, enter the number here.   `0`

    g. OPTIONAL: If you have <u>siblings, parents, or adult children</u> with the same principal residence who are combining their income with yours by submitting Form I-864A, enter the number here.   `0`

    h. Add together lines and enter the number here. **Household Size:**   `0` `2`

Part 6. Sponsor's income and employment.

22. I am currently:

    a. ☒ Employed as a/an   Plumber   .

         Name of Employer #1 *(if applicable)*   Top Quality Heating & Cooling   .

         Name of Employer #2 *(if applicable)*   .

    b. ☐ Self-employed as a/an   .

    c. ☐ Retired from   since   .
                         (Company Name)   *(Date)*

    d. ☐ Unemployed since   .
                           (Date)

23. My current individual annual income is: $ 39,000.00
                                       (See Step-by-Step Instructions)

24. My current annual household income:

    a. List your income from line 23 of this form. $ 39,000.00

    b. Income you are using from any other person who was counted in your household size, including, in certain conditions, the intending immigrant. (See step-by-step instructions.) Please indicate name, relationship and income.

Name	Relationship	Current Income
_____	_____	$ _____
_____	_____	$ _____
_____	_____	$ _____
_____	_____	$ _____

Household Size =

_____

Poverty line for year

_____ **is:**

$ _____

    c. Total Household Income: $ 39,000.00

    (Total all lines from 24a and 24b. Will be Compared to Poverty Guidelines -- See Form I-864P.)

    d. ☐ The persons listed above have completed Form I-864A. I am filing along with this form all necessary Forms I-864A completed by these persons.

    e. ☐ The person listed above, _____ does not need to
                                          (Name)
        complete Form I-864A because he/she is the intending immigrant and has no accompanying dependents.

25. Federal income tax return information.

    ☒ I have filed a Federal tax return for each of the three most recent tax years. I have attached the required photocopy or transcript of my Federal tax return for only the most recent tax year.

    My total income (adjusted gross income on IRS Form 1040EZ) as reported on my Federal tax returns for the most recent three years was:

Tax Year		Total Income
2011	*(most recent)*	$ 39,000.00
2010	*(2nd most recent)*	$ 37,000.00
2009	*(3rd most recent)*	$ 35,500.00

    ☒ *(Optional)* I have attached photocopies or transcripts of my Federal tax returns for my second and third most recent tax years.

Part 7. Use of assets to supplement income. *(Optional)*

If your income, or the total income for you and your household, from line 24c exceeds the Federal Poverty Guidelines for your household size, YOU ARE NOT REQUIRED to complete this Part. Skip to Part 8.

26. Your assets *(Optional)*

a. Enter the balance of all savings and checking accounts.

$ 1,800.00

b. Enter the net cash value of real-estate holdings. (Net means current assessed value minus mortgage debt.)

$ 8,000.00

c. Enter the net cash value of all stocks, bonds, certificates of deposit, and any other assets not already included in lines 26 (a) or (b).

$ 5,200.00

d. **Add together lines 26 a, b and c and enter the number here.**   TOTAL: $ 15,000.00

27. Your household member's assets from Form I-864A. *(Optional)*

Assets from Form I-864A, line 12d for

$ _____

(Name of Relative)

28. Assets of the principal sponsored immigrant. *(Optional)*

The principal sponsored immigrant is the person listed in line 2.

a. Enter the balance of the sponsored immigrant's savings and checking accounts.

$ 5,000.00

b. Enter the net cash value of all the sponsored immigrant's real estate holdings. (Net means investment value minus mortgage debt.)

$ 0.00

c. Enter the current cash value of the sponsored immigrant's stocks, bonds, certificates of deposit, and other assets not included on line a or b.

$ 0.00

d. **Add together lines 28a, b, and c, and enter the number here.**

$ 5,000.00

29. Total value of assets.

Add together lines 26d, 27 and 28d and enter the number here.   TOTAL: $ 20,000.00

Household Size =

_____

Poverty line for year

_____ is:

$ _____

The total value of all assests, line 29, must equal 5 times (3 times for spouses and children of USCs, or 1 time for orphans to be formally adopted in the U.S.) the difference between the poverty guidelines and the sponsor's household income, line 24c.

Part 8. Sponsor's Contract.

Please note that, by signing this Form I-864, you agree to assume certain specific obligations under the Immigration and Nationality Act and other Federal laws. The following paragraphs describe those obligations. Please read the following information carefully before you sign the Form I-864. If you do not understand the obligations, you may wish to consult an attorney or accredited representative.

What is the Legal Effect of My Signing a Form I-864?

If you sign a Form I-864 on behalf of any person (called the "intending immigrant") who is applying for an immigrant visa or for adjustment of status to a permanent resident, and that intending immigrant submits the Form I-864 to the U.S. Government with his or her application for an immigrant visa or adjustment of status, under section 213A of the Immigration and Nationality Act these actions create a contract between you and the U. S. Government. The intending immigrant's becoming a permanent resident is the "consideration" for the contract.

Under this contract, you agree that, in deciding whether the intending immigrant can establish that he or she is not inadmissible to the United States as an alien likely to become a public charge, the U.S. Government can consider your income and assets to be available for the support of the intending immigrant.

What If I choose Not to Sign a Form I-864?

You cannot be made to sign a Form 1-864 if you do not want to do so. But if you do not sign the Form I-864, the intending immigrant may not be able to become a permanent resident in the United States.

What Does Signing the Form I-864 Require Me to do?

If an intending immigrant becomes a permanent resident in the United States based on a Form I-864 that you have signed, then, until your obligations under the Form I-864 terminate, you must:

-- Provide the intending immigrant any support necessary to maintain him or her at an income that is at least 125 percent of the Federal Poverty Guidelines for his or her household size (100 percent if you are the petitioning sponsor and are on active duty in the U.S. Armed Forces and the person is your husband, wife, unmarried child under 21 years old.)

-- Notify USCIS of any change in your address, within 30 days of the change, by filing Form I-865.

What Other Consequences Are There?

If an intending immigrant becomes a permanent resident in the United States based on a Form I-864 that you have signed, then until your obligations under the Form I-864 terminate, your income and assets may be considered ("deemed") to be available to that person, in determining whether he or she is eligible for certain Federal means-tested public benefits and also for State or local means-tested public benefits, if the State or local government's rules provide for consideration ("deeming") of your income and assets as available to the person.

This provision does **not** apply to public benefits specified in section 403(c) of the Welfare Reform Act such as, but not limited to, emergency Medicaid, short-term, non-cash emergency relief; services provided under the National School Lunch and Child Nutrition Acts; immunizations and testing and treatment for communicable diseases; and means-tested programs under the Elementary and Secondary Education Act.

Contract continued on following page.

What If I Do Not Fulfill My Obligations?

If you do not provide sufficient support to the person who becomes a permanent resident based on the Form I-864 that you signed, that person may sue you for this support.

If a Federal, State or local agency, or a private agency provides any covered means-tested public benefit to the person who becomes a permanent resident based on the Form I-864 that you signed, the agency may ask you to reimburse them for the amount of the benefits they provided. If you do not make the reimbursement, the agency may sue you for the amount that the agency believes you owe.

If you are sued, and the court enters a judgment against you, the person or agency that sued you may use any legally permitted procedures for enforcing or collecting the judgment. You may also be required to pay the costs of collection, including attorney fees.

If you do not file a properly completed Form I-865 within 30 days of any change of address, USCIS may impose a civil fine for your failing to do so.

When Will These Obligations End?

Your obligations under a Form I-864 will end if the person who becomes a permanent resident based on a Form I-864 that you signed:

- Becomes a U.S. citizen;

- Has worked, or can be credited with, 40 quarters of coverage under the Social Security Act;

- No longer has lawful permanent resident status, and has departed the United States;

- Becomes subject to removal, but applies for and obtains in removal proceedings a new grant of adjustment of status, based on a new affidavit of support, if one is required; or

- Dies.

Note that divorce **does not** terminate your obligations under this Form I-864.

Your obligations under a Form I-864 also end if you die. Therefore, if you die, your Estate will not be required to take responsibility for the person's support after your death. Your Estate may, however, be responsible for any support that you owed before you died.

30. I, John Robert ADAMS ,

(Print Sponsor's Name)

certify under penalty of perjury under the laws of the United States that:

  a. I know the contents of this affidavit of support that I signed.

  b. All the factual statements in this affidavit of support are true and correct.

  c. I have read and I understand each of the obligations described in Part 8, and I agree, freely and without any mental reservation or purpose of evasion, to accept each of those obligations in order to make it possible for the immigrants indicated in Part 3 to become permanent residents of the United States;

  d. I agree to submit to the personal jurisdiction of any Federal or State court that has subject matter jurisdiction of a lawsuit against me to enforce my obligations under this Form I-864;

  e. Each of the Federal income tax returns submitted in support of this affidavit are true copies, or are unaltered tax transcripts, of the tax returns I filed with the U.S. Internal Revenue Service; and

Sign on following page.

f. I authorize the Social Security Administration to release information about me in its records to the Department of State and U.S. Citizenship and Immigration Services.

g. Any and all other evidence submitted is true and correct.

31. _____   _____

(Sponsor's Signature)   (Date-- mm/dd/yyyy)

Part 9. Information on Preparer, if prepared by someone other than the sponsor.

I certify under penalty of perjury under the laws of the United States that I prepared this affidavit of support at the sponsor's request and that this affidavit of support is based on all information of which I have knowledge.

Signature: _____   **Date:** _____

(mm/dd/yyyy)

Printed Name: _____

Firm Name: _____

Address: _____

Telephone Number: _____

E-Mail Address : _____

Business State ID # *(if any)* _____

Department of Homeland Security
U.S. Citizenship and Immigration Services

I-693, Report of Medical
Examination and Vaccination Record

START HERE - Type or print in CAPITAL letters (*Use black ink*)

Part 1. Information About You *(The person requesting a medical examination or vaccinations must complete this part)*

Family Name (Last Name)	Given Name (First Name)	Full Middle Name
ADAMS	Johanna	Gottlieb

Home Address: Street Number and Name: 789 Oak Street

Apt. Number: 33A

Gender: ☐ Male ☒ Female

City	State	Zip Code	Phone # (*Include Area Code) no dashes or ()*
New York	NY	11220	(212) 555-2591

Date of Birth *(mm/dd/yyyy)*	Place of Birth *(City/Town/Village)*	Country of Birth	A-Number *(if any)*	U.S. Social Security # *(if any)*
12/16/1980	Hamburg	Germany	876543210	147-25-8366

Applicant's Certification

I certify under penalty of perjury under United States law that I am the person who is identified in **Part 1** of this Form I-693, Report of Medical Examination and Vaccination Record, and that the information in **Part 1** of this form is true to the best of my knowledge. I understand the purpose of this medical exam, and I authorize the required tests and procedures to be completed. If it is determined that I willfully misrepresented a material fact or provided false/altered information or documents with regard to my medical exam, I understand that any immigration benefit I derived from this medical exam may be revoked, that I may be removed from the United States, and that I may be subject to civil or criminal penalties.

Signature - Do not sign or date this form until instructed to do so by the civil surgeon

Date *(mm/dd/yyyy)*

Part 2. Medical Examination *(The civil surgeon completes this part)*

1. Examination

Date of First Examination

Date(s) of Follow-up Examination(s) if Required:

Date of Exam	Date of Exam	Date of Exam

Summary of Overall Findings:

☐ No Class A or Class B Condition   ☐ Class A Conditions (see **2** through **5** below)   ☐ Class B Conditions (see **2** through **6** below)

2. Communicable Diseases of Public Health Significance

A. Tuberculosis (TB): An initial screening test, either a Tuberculin Skin Test (TST) or an Interferon Gamma Release Assay (IGRA) is required for all applicants 2 years of age and older; for children under 2 years of age, see *Technical Instructions* at **http://cdc.gov/ncidod/dq/civil.htm**. The civil surgeon should perform **one type of initial screening test only**, followed by further evaluation, if needed (chest X-ray).

1. Tuberculin Skin Test (TST):

☐ Not administered (TST exception applies)

Date TST Applied	Date TST Read	Size of Reaction *(mm)*

Result: ☐ Negative (4mm or less of induration)   ☐ Positive (≥ 5mm; chest X-ray required)

2. Interferon Gamma Release Assay (IGRA) (for acceptable IGRAs consult the Technical Instructions and any updates posted on CDC's Web site at http://www.cdc.gov/ncidod/dq/civil.htm):

☐ Not administered (IGRA exception applies)

Name of Test	Date Blood Sample Drawn

Form I-693 (Rev. 07/20/10)N

Part 2. Communicable Diseases of Public Health Significance *(Cont'd)*

IU/ml:

Result: ☐ Negative (including indeterminate, or borderline/ equivocal) (no chest X-ray required)

☐ Positive (chest X-ray required)

Initial Screening Test Result and Chest X-Ray Determination:

☐ Chest X-ray not required (medically cleared for TB for USCIS)

☐ Chest X-ray required due to TB signs or symptoms, or due to immunosuppression (e.g. HIV)

☐ Chest X-ray required due to initial screening test results

☐ Chest X-ray required due to TST or IGRA exception (The civil surgeon must clearly specify the TST or IGRA exception in the "Remarks" field below.)

----

4. Chest X-Ray: Required based on TST or IGRA result, or if specific TST or IGRA exceptions apply, or for an applicant with TB signs or symptoms or immunosuppression (e.g., HIV). Attach a copy of X-ray report.

Date Chest X-Ray Taken

Date Chest X-Ray Read

Results

☐ Normal

☐ Abnormal (Describe results in remarks.)

TB Classification/Findings (check only if chest x-ray was performed):

☐ No Class A or Class B TB ☐ Class B1 Pulmonary TB ☐ Class B2 Pulmonary TB ☐ Class B, Other Chest Condition (non-TB)

☐ Class A Pulmonary TB Disease ☐ Class B1 Extra Pulmonary TB ☐ Class B, Latent TB Infection

Remarks: (Include any signs or symptoms of TB, additional tests, and therapy given, with stop and start dates and any changes.)

B. Syphilis

☐ Serologic Test for Syphilis (Required for applicants 15 years and older)

Date Screening Run

[   ]

If Reactive, Date Confirmation Run

[   ]

☐ Screening Nonreactive

☐ Screening Reactive, Titer 1: [   ]

☐ Confirmation Nonreactive

☐ Confirmation Reactive

Findings:

☐ No Class A or Class B Syphilis

☐ Syphilis, Class A (untreated)

☐ Syphilis, Class B (with residual deficit, and treated in the past year)

Remarks: (Include any therapy given with doses and dates.)

[   ]

C. Other Class A/Class B Conditions for Communicable Diseases of Public Health Significance

Findings:

☐ No Class A/B Condition

☐ Chancroid, Class A

☐ Granuloma Inguinale, Class A

☐ Gonorrhea, Class A

☐ Lymphogranuloma Venereum, Class A

☐ Hansen's Disease (Leprosy, Infectious), Class A

☐ Hansen's Disease (Leprosy, Noninfectious), Class B

Remarks: (Include any therapy given and any counseling or referrals.)

[   ]

3. Physical or Mental Disorders With Associated Harmful Behavior

*(Include here any diagnosis of substance abuse/addiction based on DSM criteria for a substance that is **not** listed in Schedule I, II, III, IV, or V under Section 202 of the Controlled Substance Act with current associated harmful behavior or history of associated harmful behavior judged likely to recur. This category includes diagnosis of alcohol abuse/dependence.)

☐ No Class A or B Physical or Mental Disorder*

☐ Current Physical/Mental Disorder with Associated Harmful Behavior,* Class A

☐ History of Physical/Mental Disorder with Associated Harmful Behavior Likely to Recur, Class A*

☐ Current Physical/Mental Disorder without Associated Harmful Behavior,* Class B

☐ History of Physical/Mental Disorder with Associated Harmful Behavior Unlikely to Recur,* Class B

Remarks: (Include diagnosis, likelihood of recurrence of the harmful behavior, therapy given, and any counseling, or referrals. Attach a separate sheet of paper (with applicant's name and A#) if more space is necessary.)

[   ]

4. Drug Abuse/Drug Addiction

("Drug Abuse/Drug Addiction" addresses non-medical use **only with respect to substances listed in Schedule I, II, III, IV, or V under Section 202 of the Controlled Substances Act. Include here any diagnosis of substance abuse/dependence based on DSM criteria for a substance listed in Schedule I, II, III, IV, or V of section 202 of the Controlled Substances Act. See CDC's Technical Instructions posted on CDC's Web site at **http://www.cdc.gov/immigrantrefugeehealth/exams/ti/civil/technical-instructions-civil-surgeons.html.**)

☐ No Class A or B Substance (Drug) Abuse/Addiction**

☐ Substance (Drug) Abuse/Addiction, Listed in Section 202 of the Controlled Substances Act,** Class A

☐ Substance (Drug) Abuse/Addiction in Full Remission, Listed in Section 202 of the Controlled Substances Act,** Class B

Remarks: (Include any therapy given, rehabilitation, counseling, or referrals. Attach a separate sheet of paper (with applicant's name and A#) if more space is necessary.)

[   ]

5. Vaccinations (See *Technical Instructions* at **http://www.cdc.gov/ncidod/dq/civil.htm** for list of required vaccines.)

Vaccine History Transferred From a Written Record				Vaccine Given	Completed Series	Waiver(s) to Be Requested From USCIS			
						Blanket			
				Date Given by Civil Surgeon mm/dd/yy	Mark an X if completed; write date of lab test if immune or "VH" if varicella history		Not Medically Appropriate		
Vaccine	Date Received mm/dd/yy	Date Received mm/dd/yy	Date Received mm/dd/yy			Not Age Appropriate	Contra-indication	Insufficient Time Interval	Not Flu Season
Specify Vaccine: DT ☐ DTP ☐ DTaP ☐									■
Specify Vaccine: Td ☐ Tdap ☐									■
Specify Vaccine: OPV ☐ IPV ☐									■
MMR (Measles Mumps-Rubella) or if monovalent or other combination of the vaccines are given, specify vaccine(s):									■
Hib									■
Hepatitis B									■
Varicella									■
Pneumococcal									■
Influenza									
Rotavirus									■
Hepatitis A									■
Meningococcal									■

Results:

Give Copy to Applicant

☐ Applicant may be eligible for blanket waiver(s) as indicated above.
☐ Applicant will request an individual waiver based on religious or moral convictions.
☐ Vaccine history complete for each vaccine, all requirements met.
☐ Applicant does not meet immunization requirements.

Name of Applicant

A-Number *(if any)*

Remarks: *(If needed, provide any remarks; e.g., reason for contraindication)*

Part 2. Medical Examination *(Continued)*

6. List other medical conditions, Class B other (e.g., hypertension, diabetes)

Part 3. Referral to Health Department Other Doctor/Facility *(To be completed by civil surgeon, if referral was required and made)*

Type or Print Name of Doctor or Health Department Receiving Required Referral

Date of Referral *(mm/dd/yyyy)*

Address: (Street Number and Name, City, State, and Zip Code)

Daytime Phone # *(Include Area Code) no dashes or ( )*

Remarks: (Include name of medical condition and reasons for referral.)

Part 4. To Be Completed by Physician Or Health Department Performing Referral Evaluation

The applicant identified on this form was referred to me by the civil surgeon named in **Part 5** of this form. I have provided appropriate evaluation/treatment, having made every reasonable effort to verify that the person whom I evaluated/treated is the person identified in **Part 1**.

Type or Print Full Name of Evaluating Physician or Health Department

Signature

Address: (Street Number and Name, City, State, and Zip Code)

Date *(mm/dd/yyyy)*

Name of Medical Practice or Health Department

Daytime Phone # *(Include Area Code) no dashes or ( )*

Remarks: (Attach a separate sheet of paper, if needed.)

Part 5.   Civil Surgeon's Certification *(Do not sign form or have the applicant sign in Part 1 until all health follow-up requirements have been met.)*

I certify under penalty of perjury under United States law that: I am a civil surgeon in current status designated to examine applicants seeking certain immigration benefits in the United States; I have a currently valid and unrestricted license to practice medicine in the state where I am performing medical examinations; I performed this examination of the person identified in **Part 1** of this Form I-693, after having made every reasonable effort to verify that person whom I examined is the person identified in **Part 1**; that I performed the examination in accordance with the Centers for Disease Control and Prevention's *Technical Instructions*, and all supplemental information or updates; and that all information provided by me on this form is true and correct to the best of my knowledge, and belief.

Type or Print Full Name   *(First, Middle, Last)*

Signature

Address (Street Number and Name, City, State, and Zip Code)

Date *(mm/dd/yyyy)*

Name of Medical Practice or Health Department

Daytime Phone # *(Include Area Code) no dashes or ( )*

E-Mail Address

Part 6.   Health Department Identifying Information *(If completed by State or local health department on behalf of a refugee, place a stamp or seal where indicated.)*

Type or Print Name

(Place State or local health department stamp/seal below.)

Signature

Date *(mm/dd/yyyy)*

Daytime Phone # *(Include Area Code) no dashes or ( )*

Part 7.   For USCIS Use Only *(Not to be completed by the civil surgeon)*

☐ 212(g)(2)(B) Blanket Waiver for Vaccination Granted

Remarks (if needed):

OMB No. 1615-0040; Expires 09/30/2011

Department of Homeland Security
U.S. Citizenship and Immigration Services

I-765, Application For
Employment Authorization

Do not write in this block.

Remarks	Action Block	Fee Stamp
A#		
Applicant is filing under §274a.12 _____		

☐ Application Approved. Employment Authorized / Extended *(Circle One)*   until _____ (Date).
_____ (Date).

    Subject to the following conditions: _____
    Application Denied.
      ☐ Failed to establish eligibility under 8 CFR 274a.12 (a) or (c).
      ☐ Failed to establish economic necessity as required in 8 CFR 274a.12(c)(14), (18) and 8 CFR 214.2(f)

I am applying for: ☒ Permission to accept employment.
            ☐ Replacement *(of lost employment authorization document)*.
            ☐ Renewal of my permission to accept employment *(attach previous employment authorization document)*.

1. Name (Family Name in CAPS) (First) (Middle)
ADAMS   Johanna   Gottlieb

Which USCIS Office?   Date(s)

2. Other Names Used (include Maiden Name)
GOTTLIEB

Results (Granted or Denied - attach all documentation)

3. Address in the United States (Number and Street)   (Apt. Number)
789 Oak Street   33A

12. Date of Last Entry into the U.S. (mm/dd/yyyy)
11/20/2009

(Town or City) (State/Country) (ZIP Code)
New York   NY   11220

13. Place of Last Entry into the U.S.
New York

4. Country of Citizenship/Nationality
Germany

14. Manner of Last Entry (Visitor, Student, etc.)
K-3

5. Place of Birth (Town or City) (State/Province) (Country)
Hamburg   Germany

15. Current Immigration Status (Visitor, Student, etc.)
K-3

6. Date of Birth (mm/dd/yyyy)
12/16/1980

7. Gender
☐ Male ☒ Female

16. Go to **Part 2** of the Instructions, Eligibility Categories. In the space below, place the letter and number of the category you selected from the instructions (For example, (a)(8), (c)(17)(iii), etc.).

8. Marital Status   ☒ Married   ☐ Single
                ☐ Widowed   ☐ Divorced

Eligibility under 8 CFR 274a.12 (   ) (C) (9)

9. Social Security Number (include all numbers you have ever used) (if any)
147-25-8369

17. If you entered the Eligibility Category, (c)(3)(C), in item 16 above, list your degree, your employer's name as listed in E-Verify, and your employer's E-Verify Company Identification Number or a valid E-Verify Client Company Identification Number in the space below.

10. Alien Registration Number (A-Number) or I-94 Number (if any)
876-543-210

Degree: _____

11. Have you ever before applied for employment authorization from USCIS?
   ☐ Yes (If "Yes," complete below)   ☐ No

Employer's Name as listed in E-Verify: _____

Employer's E-Verify Company Identification Number or a valid E-Verify Client Company Identification Number _____

Certification

Your Certification: I certify, under penalty of perjury under the laws of the United States of America, that the foregoing is true and correct. Furthermore, I authorize the release of any information that U.S. Citizenship and Immigration Services needs to determine eligibility for the benefit I am seeking. I have read the Instructions in **Part 2** and have identified the appropriate eligibility category in **Block 16**.

Signature	Telephone Number	Date
	(212) 555-2591	

Signature of Person Preparing Form, If Other Than Above: I declare that this document was prepared by me at the request of the applicant and is based on all information of which I have any knowledge.

Print Name	Address	*Signature*	Date

Remarks	Initial Receipt	Resubmitted	Relocated		Completed		
			Rec'd	Sent	Approved	Denied	Returned

Form I-765 (Rev. 11/23/10)Y

DO NOT WRITE IN THIS BLOCK		FOR USCIS USE ONLY (except G-28 block below)

Document Issued
- ☐ Reentry Permit
- ☐ Refugee Travel Document
- ☐ Single Advance Parole
- ☐ Multiple Advance Parole
  Valid to: _____

If Reentry Permit or Refugee Travel Document, mail to:
- ☐ Address in Part 1
- ☐ U.S. Embassy/consulate at: _____
- ☐ Overseas DHS office at: _____

Action Block

Receipt

☐ Document Hand Delivered

On _____ By _____

To be completed by Attorney/Representative, if any.
Attorney State License # _____

☐ Check box if G-28 is attached.

Part 1. Information About You *(Type or print in black ink)*

1. A Number
876543210

2. Date of Birth *(mm/dd/yyyy)*
12/16/1980

3. Class of Admission
K-3

4. Gender
☐ Male ☒ Female

5. Name *(Family name in capital letters)* / *(First)* / *(Middle)*

ADAMS	Johanna	Gottlieb

6. Address *(Number and Street)*
789 Oak Street

Apt. Number
33A

City: New York

State or Province: NY

Zip/Postal Code: 11220

Country: USA

7. Country of Birth
Germany

8. Country of Citizenship
Germany

9. Social Security # *(if any)*
147-25-8369

Part 2. Application Type *(Check one)*

a. ☐ I am a permanent resident or conditional resident of the United States, and I am applying for a reentry permit.

b. ☐ I now hold U.S. refugee or asylee status, and I am applying for a Refugee Travel Document.

c. ☐ I am a permanent resident as a direct result of refugee or asylee status, and I am applying for a Refugee Travel Document.

d. ☒ I am applying for an advance parole document to allow me to return to the United States after temporary foreign travel.

e. ☐ I am outside the United States, and I am applying for an Advance Parole Document.

f. ☐ I am applying for an Advance Parole Document for a person who is outside the United States. *If you checked box "f," provide the following information about that person:*

1. Name *(Family name in capital letters)* / *(First)* / *(Middle)*

2. Date of Birth *(mm/dd/yyyy)*

3. Country of Birth

4. Country of Citizenship

5. Address *(Number and Street)* — Apt. # — Daytime Telephone # *(area/country code)*

City — State or Province — Zip/Postal Code — Country

Part 3. Processing Information

1. Date of Intended Departure *(mm/dd/yyyy)*

05/15/2011

2. Expected Length of Trip

2 Weeks

3. Are you, or any person included in this application, now in exclusion, deportation, removal, or rescission proceedings? ☐ Yes ☒ No *(Name of DHS office)*:

If you are applying for an Advance Parole Document, skip to Part 7.

4. Have you ever before been issued a reentry permit or Refugee Travel Document?

☐ No ☐ Yes *(If "Yes," give the following information for the last document issued to you)*:

Date Issued *(mm/dd/yyyy)*:

Disposition *(attached, lost, etc.)*:

5. Where do you want this travel document sent? *(Check one)*

a. ☐ To the U.S. address shown in **Part 1** on the first page of this form.

b. ☐ To a U.S. Embassy or consulate at: City: Country:

c. ☐ To a DHS office overseas at: City: Country:

d. If you checked "b" or "c," where should the notice to pick up the travel document be sent?

☐ To the address shown in **Part 2** on the first page of this form.

☐ To the address shown below:

Address *(Number and Street)* | Apt. # | Daytime Telephone # *(area/country code)*

City | State or Province | Zip/Postal Code | Country

Part 4. Information About Your Proposed Travel

Purpose of trip. *(If you need more room, continue on a separate sheet of paper.)*	List the countries you intend to visit.

Part 5. Complete Only If Applying for a Reentry Permit

Since becoming a permanent resident of the United States (or during the past five years, whichever is less) how much total time have you spent outside the United States?	☐ less than six months ☐ two to three years ☐ six months to one year ☐ three to four years ☐ one to two years ☐ more than four years

Since you became a permanent resident of the United States, have you ever filed a Federal income tax return as a nonresident or failed to file a Federal income tax return because you considered yourself to be a nonresident? *(If "Yes," give details on a separate sheet of paper.)* ☐ Yes ☐ No

Part 6. Complete Only If Applying for a Refugee Travel Document

1. Country from which you are a refugee or asylee:

If you answer "Yes" to any of the following questions, you must explain on a separate sheet of paper.

2. Do you plan to travel to the country named above? ☐ Yes ☐ No

3. Since you were accorded refugee/asylee status, have you ever:

a. Returned to the country named above? ☐ Yes ☐ No

b. Applied for and/or obtained a national passport, passport renewal, or entry permit of that country? ☐ Yes ☐ No

c. Applied for and/or received any benefit from such country (for example, health insurance benefits). ☐ Yes ☐ No

4. Since you were accorded refugee/asylee status, have you, by any legal procedure or voluntary act:

a. Reacquired the nationality of the country named above? ☐ Yes ☐ No

b. Acquired a new nationality? ☐ Yes ☐ No

c. Been granted refugee or asylee status in any other country? ☐ Yes ☐ No

Part 7. Complete Only If Applying for Advance Parole

On a separate sheet of paper, explain how you qualify for an Advance Parole Document, and what circumstances warrant issuance of advance parole. Include copies of any documents you wish considered. *(See instructions.)*

1. How many trips do you intend to use this document? ☐ One Trip ☒ More than one trip

2. If the person intended to receive an Advance Parole Document is outside the United States, provide the location (city and country) of the U.S. Embassy or consulate or the DHS overseas office that you want us to notify.

City

| Hamburg (or leave blank) |

Country

| Germany |

3. If the travel document will be delivered to an overseas office, where should the notice to pick up the document be sent?:

☐ To the address shown in **Part 2** on the first page of this form.

☒ To the address shown below:

Address *(Number and Street)*   Apt. #   Daytime Telephone # *(area/country code)*

| Enter your foreign address (if applicable) | | |

City   State or Province   Zip/Postal Code   Country

| | | | |

Part 8. Signature   *Read the information on penalties in the instructions before completing this section. If you are filing for a reentry permit or Refugee Travel Document, you must be in the United States to file this application.*

I certify, under penalty of perjury under the laws of the United States of America, that this application and the evidence submitted with it are all true and correct. I authorize the release of any information from my records that U.S. Citizenship and Immigration Services needs to determine eligibility for the benefit I am seeking.

Signature   Date *(mm/dd/yyyy)*   Daytime Telephone Number *(with area code)*

| | | |

Note: If you do not completely fill out this form or fail to submit required documents listed in the instructions, you may not be found eligible for the requested document and this application may be denied.

Part 9. Signature of Person Preparing Form, If Other Than the Applicant *(Sign below)*

I declare that I prepared this application at the request of the applicant, and it is based on all information of which I have knowledge.

Signature   Print or Type Your Name

| | |

Firm Name and Address   Daytime Telephone Number *(with area code)*

| | |

Fax Number *(if any)*   Date *(mm/dd/yyyy)*

| | |

Department of Homeland Security
U.S. Citizenship and Immigration Services

I-751, Petition to Remove Conditions on Residence

START HERE - Type or print in black ink.

Part 1. Information About You

Family Name (Last Name)
ADAMS

Given Name (First Name)
Joanna

Full Middle Name
Gottlieb

Address: (Street Number and Name)
789 Oak Street

Apt. #
33A

C/O: (In care of)

City
New York

State/Province
NY

Country
USA

Zip/Postal Code
11220

Mailing Address, if different than above (Street Number and Name):
SAME

Apt. #

C/O: (In care of)

City

State/Province

Country

Zip/Postal Code

Date of Birth (mm/dd/yyyy)
12/16/1980

Country of Birth
Germany

Country of Citizenship
Germany

Alien Registration Number (A-Number)
876-543-210

Social Security # (if any)
147-25-8369

Conditional Residence Expires on (mm/dd/yyyy)
01/24/2013

Daytime Phone # (Area/Country Code)
(212) 555-2591

For USCIS Use Only

Returned	Receipt
Date	
Date	
Resubmitted	
Date	
Date	
Reloc Sent	
Date	
Date	
Reloc Rec'd	
Date	
Date	
☐ Petitioner Interviewed on _____	

Remarks

Action Block

To Be Completed by
Attorney or Representative, if any
☐ Fill in box if Form G-28 is attached to represent the applicant.

ATTY State License #

Part 2. Basis for Petition (Check one)

a. ☒ My conditional residence is based on my marriage to a U.S. citizen or permanent resident, and we are filing this petition together.

b. ☐ I am a child who entered as a conditional permanent resident, and I am unable to be included in a joint petition filed by my parent(s).

OR

My conditional residence is based on my marriage to a U.S. citizen or permanent resident, I am unable to file a joint petition, and I request a waiver because: **(Check one)**

c. ☐ My spouse is deceased.

d. ☐ I entered into the marriage in good faith, but the marriage was terminated through divorce or annulment.

e. ☐ I am a conditional resident spouse who entered a marriage in good faith, and during the marriage I was battered by or was the subject of extreme cruelty by my U.S. citizen or permanent resident spouse or parent.

f. ☐ I am a conditional resident child who was battered by or subjected to extreme cruelty by my U.S. citizen or conditional resident parent(s).

g. ☐ The termination of my status and removal from the United States would result in an extreme hardship.

Form I-751 (Rev. 11/23/10) Y

Part 3. Additional Information About You

1. Other Names Used *(including maiden name)*:

> GOTTLIEB (maiden)

2. Date of Marriage *(mm/dd/yyyy)*	**3.** Place of Marriage	**4.** If your spouse is deceased, give the date of death *(mm/dd/yyyy)*
02/14/2009	Reno, NV, USA	n/a

5. Are you in removal, deportation, or rescission proceedings?	☐ Yes	☒ No
6. Was a fee paid to anyone other than an attorney in connection with this petition?	☐ Yes	☒ No
7. Have you ever been arrested, detained, charged, indicted, fined, or imprisoned for breaking or violating any law or ordinance (excluding traffic regulations), or committed any crime which you were not arrested in the United States or abroad?	☐ Yes	☒ No
8. If you are married, is this a different marriage than the one through which conditional residence status was obtained?	☐ Yes	☒ No
9. Have you resided at any other address since you became a permanent resident? *(If "Yes," attach a list of all addresses and dates.)*	☐ Yes	☒ No
10. Is your spouse currently serving with or employed by the U.S. Government and serving outside the United States?	☐ Yes	☒ No

If you answered "Yes" to any of the above, provide a detailed explanation on a separate sheet of paper and refer to "What Initial Evidence Is Required?" to determine what criminal history documentation to include with your petition. Place your name and A-Number at the top of each sheet and give the number of the item that refers to your response.

Part 4. Information About the Spouse or Parent Through Whom You Gained Your Conditional Residence

Family Name	First Name	Middle Name
ADAMS	John	Robert

Address

> 789 Oak Street, Apt. 33A New York, NY 11220

Date of Birth *(mm/dd/yyyy)*	Social Security # *(if any)*	A-Number *(if any)*
06/21/1978	012-34-5678	None

Part 5. Information About Your Children-List All Your Children *(Attach other sheets if necessary)*

Name *(First/Middle/Last)*	Date of Birth *(mm/dd/yyyy)*	A-Number *(if any)*	If in U.S., give address/immigration status	Living with you?
None				☐ Yes ☐ No
				☐ Yes ☐ No
				☐ Yes ☐ No
				☐ Yes ☐ No
				☐ Yes ☐ No

Part 6. Accommodations for Individuals With Disabilities and Impairments *(Read the information in the instructions before completing this section.)*

I am requesting an accommodation:

1. Because of my disability(ies) and/or impairment(s).	☐ Yes	☒ No
2. For my spouse because of his or her disability(ies) and/or impairment(s).	☐ Yes	☒ No
3. For my included child(ren) because of his or her (their) disability(ies) and/or impairment(s).	☐ Yes	☒ No

If you answered "Yes," check any applicable box. Provide information on the disability(ies) and/or impairment(s) for each person:

☐ Deaf or hard of hearing and request the following accommodation(s) (if requesting a sign-language interpreter, indicate which language (e.g., American Sign Language)):

_____

☐ Blind or sight-impaired and request the following accommodation(s):

_____

☐ Other type of disability(ies) and/or impairment(s) (describe the nature of the disability(ies) and/or impairment(s) and accommodation(s) being requested):

_____

Part 7. Signature

(Read the information on penalties on Page 5 of the instructions before completing this section. If you checked block "a" in Part 2, your spouse must also sign below).

I certify, under penalty of perjury of the laws of the United States of America, that this petition and the evidence submitted with it is all true and correct. If conditional residence was based on a marriage, I further certify that the marriage was entered in accordance with the laws of the place where the marriage took place and was not for the purpose of procuring an immigration benefit. I also authorize the release of any information from my records that U.S. Citizenship and Immigration Services needs to determine eligibility for the benefit sought.

Signature	Print Name	Date *(mm/dd/yyyy)*

Signature of Spouse	Print Name	Date *(mm/dd/yyyy)*

NOTE: If you do not completely fill out this form or fail to submit any required documents listed in the instructions, you may not be found eligible for the requested benefit and this petition may be denied.

Part 8. Signature of Person Preparing Form, If Other than Above

I declare that I prepared this petition at the request of the above person, and it is based on all information of which I have knowledge.

Signature	Print Name	Date *(mm/dd/yyyy)*

Firm Name and Address

Daytime Phone Number
(Area/Country Code)

E-Mail Address
(if any)

Part Four: TEMPLATES

Part Four: TEMPLATES

Contents

The seven templates included here will save you time. Replace all the bracketed info with your own info and modify the model as needed.

Templates

CONTINUATION SHEET TEMPLATE

[Form]
[U.S. Citizen or Alien Name]
[Alien Number] (if any)
[Social Security Number] (if any)

<u>Continuation Sheet [A, B, C etc.]</u>

[Form] [Part/Section], [Question Number (and letter)]

[Enter complete USCIS question]

[Answer question]

[Signature and Date]

TRANSLATOR CERTIFICATION TEMPLATE

Include in front of each translated document

Translator Certification

I [name] certify that I am fluent in English and [other language], and that the attached document is an accurate translation of [the foreign spouse's full name] [foreign spouse's Alien Number] [name of document].

Signature _____Date_____

[Typed Name of Translator]
[Address]
[Phone Number]

SWORN AFFIDAVIT FOR FROM I-130 & I-751 TEMPLATE

BEFORE THE UNITED STATES CITIZENSHIP & IMMIGRATION SERVICES
UNITED STATES DEPARTMENT OF HOMELAND SECURITY

<u>Affidavit of [Name of Author] on the Bona Fides of the Marriage of</u>
[Foreign Spouse's Name, Alien Number] and
U.S. Citizen [Name]

To Whom It May Concern,

My name is [...] I live at [...]. I was born in [...] on [...]. I am a [title] at [organization,]. This is written regarding my observation that [...] and [...] live happily together as husband and wife. I have been [name's] [relationship] since [date]. I have spent time with [names'] wife/husband, [name], on numerous occasions, particularly [when or where]. I can attest that they are not only married, but that they have a sound and stable marriage.

Please feel free to contact me if I can be of further assistance in this matter.

Thank you for your consideration.

Sincerely,

[Signature] [Date]
[Typed name]
[Address]
[Phone number]

EMPLOYER LETTER FOR FROM I-864 TEMPLATE

Printed on employer letterhead

To whom it may concern,

[First Name, last name] has been employed full-time with the ABC Company since [yyyy] as a [Job Title], and is an employee in good standing with an annual salary of $[....].

Signed,

[Employer's Name], [Title]
[Company Name]
[Address]
[Phone Number]

ADVANCE PAROLE LETTER TEMPLATE

U.S. Citizenship and Immigration Services
P.O. Box 805887
Chicago, IL 60680-4120

RE: I-131 Request for Advance Parole by [foreign spouse's name, Alien Number]
    Co-filing with I-485 [or, if filing separately, include I-485 filing receipt/NOA.]

Dear Sir or Madam,

I respectfully request a multiple entry Advance Parole to allow me to re-enter the U.S. after temporary foreign travel.

My U.S. citizen [husband or wife] and I would like to visit my home country to visit my parents while my application for Adjustment of Status is being approved.

Please contact me if you have any questions.

Sincerely,

[Signature] [Date]
[Typed name]
[Address]
[Phone number]

INITIAL COVER LETTER TEMPLATE

ORIGINAL SUBMISSION BY

[Foreign Spouse's Full Name]

[Alien Number]

[Date of Birth]

[Date]

Dear USCIS Examiner,

In this packet, you will find following forms with all required documentation:

Form I-130

    a) Filing Fee
    b) G-325A (Alien Spouse)
    c) G-325A (U.S. Citizen)

Form I-485

    a) Filing Fee
    b) G-325A Alien
    c) I-864
    d) I-693
    e) I-765
    f) I-131

Thank you for your consideration.

Sincerely,

[First Name] [Last Name] _____Date_____

[First Name] [Last Name] _____Date_____

I-751 COVER LETTER TEMPLATE

USCIS [City] Service Center
[Full USCIS Address]

[Date]
Re: Petition to Remove Conditions on Residence
[Alien Number]
[Foreign Spouse's Full Name]
[Date of Birth]

Dear USCIS Examiner,

In this packet, you will find my Petition to Remove Conditions on Residence with the following documentation:

- Form I-751
- Check for I-751 Filing Fee
- Copy of Green Card
- Copy of Passport
- Evidence of a bona fide marriage with my U.S. citizen spouse, [Name], organized into the following categories:
    I. Proof of joint residence
    II. Family photographs
    III. Comingling of financial liability and assets
        a) Jointly filed Federal Tax Returns for [Year]
        b) [name of bank] joint checking and savings account ·
        c) Joint utility Bills
        d) Lease/mortgage for our shared residence
        e) Joint Cellular Phone Bills

    IV. Affidavits by two individuals with personal knowledge or our marriage and relationship:
        a) Sworn affidavit by [Name]
        b) Sworn affidavit by [Name]

    V. Joint insurance benefits
        a) Joint [Company Name] health insurance
        b) Shared [Company Name] Insurance motor vehicle insurance
        c) Shared [Company Name] Dental Insurance with cancelled check

    VI. Miscellaneous
        a) Copy of airline tickets for our vacation to [Location] (mm/dd/yyyy – mm/dd/yyyy)
        b) Copy of [Company/Organization Name] Member cards showing joint membership

Thank you for your consideration.
Sincerely,

[First Name] [Last Name] _____Date_____

[First Name] [Last Name] _____Date_____

MARCUS CAMPANA lives and works in Durham, North Carolina.

He applied for and received a marriage based green card for his wife Mayumi in 2010. He is currently a PhD candidate at Duke University.

★

ZEPHYRUS MEDIA

17973298R00085

Made in the USA
Middletown, DE
18 February 2015